Community-Owned Knowledge

This book is part of the Peter Lang Education list.
Every volume is peer reviewed and meets
the highest quality standards for content and production.

PETER LANG
New York • Bern • Berlin
Brussels • Vienna • Oxford • Warsaw

Gilberto Arriaza and Lyn Scott

Community-Owned Knowledge

The Promise of Collaborative Action Research

PETER LANG
New York • Bern • Berlin
Brussels • Vienna • Oxford • Warsaw

Library of Congress Cataloging-in-Publication Control Number: 2021016694

Bibliographic information published by **Die Deutsche Nationalbibliothek**.
Die Deutsche Nationalbibliothek lists this publication in the "Deutsche Nationalbibliografie"; detailed bibliographic data are available on the Internet at http://dnb.d-nb.de/.

ISBN 978-1-4331-8901-2 (hardcover)
ISBN 978-1-4331-8897-8 (paperback)
ISBN 978-1-4331-8898-5 (ebook pdf)
ISBN 978-1-4331-8899-2 (epub)
ISBN 978-1-4331-8900-5 (mobi)
DOI 10.3726/b18449

© 2022 Peter Lang Publishing, Inc., New York
80 Broad Street, 5th floor, New York, NY 10004
www.peterlang.com

All rights reserved.
Reprint or reproduction, even partially, in all forms such as microfilm, xerography, microfiche, microcard, and offset strictly prohibited.

We humbly dedicate this book to the scientific community that incessantly pulls us all out from the depths of ignorance.

We Gon' Be Alright
By G.T. Reyes

My beautiful peoples
Y'all remember when Kendrick said he went to war last night
Well I think
we go to war every day and it's similar kinda fight
smog so thick—hard to see—obscured sight
Blanketing our body
Restricted movement—no might
Yet we might
put a smile on our face to fein we a'ight
despite
slippin and sliding
the jab, cross, hook of our public health blight
the jab, jab, cross of suffocating fires burning day and night
the body shot, hook of high stakes distance learning with no end in sight
the monster overhand right of white
supremacy
thwarting off assaults to annihilate our legacy
I know some folks might feel safer
if they could put hennesssey
Into our hands to comfort their jealousy
To drown out our clarity
To erase our memory
To break us mentally
To manipulate us emotionally
To distract our solidarity
To subordinate our authority
To pathologize and paint us with inferiority
lemme see
We gon' have to turn all that down emphatically
Cuz see
many don't realize some of our journeys
to be seen
heard
felt
as fully human
let alone educational leader
has not been easy
it has not
"I don't feel safe" has been weaponized
Like a gun shot

Asking critical questions
Fires back retaliation like bird shot
Microaggression spreading pellets
meant to cripple our train of thought
Make us second guess ourselves
like a never ending after thought
White emotionality and fragility got us cuffed
Like it was our fault
Rationalizing its behavior
without acknowledging its blind spots
The exhaustion makes me wish I was a robot
But I'm not
We're not
So let us draw upon our ancestors to remind us of what we've been taught
Plots to eradicate us will be overwrought
With resistance like a grape boycott
With radical imagination to give our future a better shot
our liberatory school of thought
Has prepared us for this onslaught
As fatiguing as it is
Trust in your training and your continued journey
Strengthen & uplift your beloved community
And beware the allure of capitalism and neoliberal fantasies
That trick us into thinking that we have to be
Inauthentically who we BE
How we BE
Cuz leadership is more than what we DO
It is also in how we BE
So let us be
Let us be we
And let us become
the divine selves
we were meant to be
no, That we already are
Our time is now
The fire next time
Is the fire now
Let's keep our aim in clear sight

And remember Kendrick?
He went to war last night
But he also said
we gon be alright
what

we gon be alright
come on
we gon be alright
do you hear me do you feel me
we gon be alright

Contents

List of Illustrations	xiii
List of Tables	xv
Foreword	xvii
Preface	xxi
Acknowledgments	xxiii
Introduction	1

1   The Concept   7
    Nature of Collaborative Action Research   8
        Core Components   10
        Agency and Agents   13
    The Value of Collaboration   15
        Collaboration Is Socially Situated   15
        Principal and Support Teams   16
        Collaboration within and across Disciplines   19
    Action and Social and Cultural Capital   24
        Action   24
        Social and Cultural Capital   26

		Key Chapter Learning	30
		Essential Questions	31
		Activity	32
		Resources	33
	2	The Challenge	35
		CAR, Culture, Climate, and Structure	36
		The Focal Issue	38
		Identification: Learning and Cultural Habits	41
		Situating the Issue	49
		The Action	54
		Evidence	59
		Attribution	62
		Fallacies	65
		Key Chapter Learning	67
		Essential Questions	68
		Activity	68
		Resources	70
	3	The Question	73
		The Research Question	74
		Summarizing the Challenge	74
		Examining the Factors within the Challenge	75
		Building Consensus	75
		Asking What-How Questions	75
		Operationalizing of the Research Question	77
		Variables	79
		Factors	79
		Items	80
		Question Design	81
		Define the Question	81
		Operationalize the Question	82
		Measure the Question	82
		Build Reliability in a Question	83
		Build Validity in a Question	84
		Questions at the Ground Level	84
		Ten Pitfalls to Avoid in Formulating Questions	86
		Key Chapter Learning	88

		Contents	xi

	Essential Questions	89
	Activity	90
	Resources	91
4	**What Is Known and What Is Possible**	**93**
	Sources of Information	94
	Identifying Sources	94
	Access to Sources	98
	Credibility of Sources	98
	Diversity of Source Authors	100
	The Literature Review	101
	Peer-Reviewed, Published Research	103
	Developing a System to Manage What Is Known	106
	Building Tables to Summarize the Literature	107
	Keeping a Table of Definitions	107
	Managing Time	108
	Search Basics	108
	Becoming Familiar with Online Databases	109
	Using Descriptors	111
	Maintaining a List of References	113
	Reading and Analyzing Published Information	113
	Notetaking and Annotations	114
	Writing the Literature Review	117
	Revising the Literature Review	121
	Key Chapter Learning	122
	Essential Questions	122
	Activity	123
	Resources	123
5	**The Method**	**127**
	Features of Qualitative Methodology	129
	Data Strength	131
	Data Collection and Organization	137
	Observation	137
	Observation Steps	139
	Participant Observer	140
	Field Notes	141
	Interviews	148

	Wording Questions	149
	Types of Questions	150
	Piloting the Questionnaire	150
	Varieties of Interviews	151
	Conducting the Interview	152
	Shadowing	152
	Key Chapter Learning	154
	Essential Question	155
	Activity	155
	Resources	163
6	The Analysis	165
	Data Reduction	167
	Chunking	168
	Slicing	169
	Coding	169
	Grouping	172
	Categorizing	173
	Themes	174
	Tracking Reduction	174
	Data Display	175
	Inspiring Quotations	176
	Supportive Statements	177
	Evidentiary Material	177
	Vignettes	179
	Profiles	180
	Composites	182
	Quantifying Words	183
	Bringing It All Together: Reporting Findings	184
	Organizing Findings around the Research Question	185
	Organizing Findings around Themes	185
	Executive Summary	186
	Key Chapter Learning	190
	Essential Question	191
	Activity	191
	Resources	194

Index   197

List of Illustrations

Chapter 1

Figure 1.1:	Five steps of collaborative action research	10
Figure 1.2:	The four lanes of collaborative action research methodology	12
Figure 1.3:	Group development model	17
Figure 1.4:	Social web	18
Figure 1.5:	Intradisciplinary	22
Figure 1.6:	Interdisciplinary	22
Figure 1.7:	Transdisciplinary	23

Chapter 2

Figure 2.1:	Double loop learning	41
Figure 2.2:	Gap analysis	44
Figure 2.3:	Smarter balanced results	54
Figure 2.4:	Theory of action	56
Figure 2.5:	Our theory of action	59
Figure 2.6:	Locating intrinsic factors	64
Figure 2.7:	English language arts/literacy achievement level distribution	69

Chapter 3

Figure 3.1:	Research question creation process	74
Figure 3.2:	Research question (birds-eye view) components at ground level	77
Figure 3.3:	Operationalizing the question	78
Figure 3.4:	Question design steps	81

Chapter 4

Figure 4.1:	Oral history documentation process	97
Figure 4.2:	Research article format example	103
Figure 4.3:	Formulating a search with descriptors	111
Figure 4.4:	Reading a research article	114
Figure 4.5:	Writing process of a literature review	118

Chapter 6

Figure 6.1:	Data reduction steps	167
Figure 6.2:	Data reduction steps	175

List of Tables

Chapter 1

Table 1.1:   Pre- and Post-Reading Test   30

Chapter 3

Table 3.1:   Writing Rubric (Ages 8–10)   83

Chapter 4

Table 4.1:   Sources of Information and Access   95
Table 4.2:   Research Table of Study Type, Description, and Key Findings 106
Table 4.3:   Research Methods Table   107
Table 4.4:   Literature Review Schedule   108
Table 4.5:   Features of Research Studies and Methods   115
Table 4.6:   Parts of an Annotated Bibliography   117
Table 4.7:   Mapping the Literature to the Study   118
Table 4.8:   Mechanics of the Literature Review   121

Table 4.9:	Empirical Studies Organizer	123
Table 4.10:	Theoretical Studies Organizer	124
Table 4.11:	Parts of an Annotated Bibliography	124
Table 4.12:	Mapping the Literature to the Study	124

Chapter 5

Table 5.1:	Observation Template	141
Table 5.2:	Observation and Memo Template	142
Table 5.3:	Shadowing Field Notes	153
Table 5.4:	Shadowing Summary	154

Chapter 6

Table 6.1:	Code-Key	170
Table 6.2:	Coding Template	170
Table 6.3:	Data Tracking Contact Sheet	172
Table 6.4:	Reduction Map	174
Table 6.5:	Composite Matrix	183
Table 6.6:	Frequency Analysis	184

Foreword
By Tony Smith*

You are holding an invitation. This book is an opportunity to claim a most precious gift; use it to make a difference. Your voice, your insight, and your experience have immense value and the authors of *Community-Owned Knowledge: The Promise of Collaborative Action Research* want the world to benefit from what you know. By sharing examples of people reflecting on their practice, considering evidence, and asking questions about what they are seeing, they help us practice inquiry as we read along. The authors believe there is value in learning by observing and pitching in and that knowledge that helps the community is coproduced. They explicitly deconstruct existing structures in an attempt to produce new entry points for all practitioners to share what they are doing. The book is both technical and adaptive in its portrayal of doing and sharing collaborative action research (CAR) that produces more harmony and belonging.

There have been other books about collaborative action research. Something that makes this effort special is that it is an expression of deep care for the wisdom of practitioners everywhere. What you know and do in your daily practice has immense value. Something you will see as you read this book is that when you work with others in CAR communities of practice, you begin to grow collaborative capital in the process and that energy can create systemic transformation. The experience of people living in social and material conditions working to understand and change the world takes center stage in this book. Peeling back the layers of our own assumptions allows us to see new ways to meet challenges and increase authentic belonging. Beyond recognizing the centrality of practitioners, the book demystifies the process of producing "scholarship" that can impact a broader audience.

This is a practical, theoretically informed, how-to guide for anyone who wants to share their work to make a difference in their community and beyond. Being public with competing and sometimes conflicting versions of solving complex human problems helps us all see new possibilities and potential avenues to equity and justice. The into, through, and beyond cycle that we see practiced in these pages helps build the discipline to look at all of our work as reproducing or transforming our conditions. Desire to change outcomes is important and, as we will see, insufficient. We need new tools to do new work, and there are many concrete "how to's" and tools in the following pages. The inclusive mixed-methodology CAR the authors describe here helps pull back the curtain on the underlying structures that both constrain and afford possible actions. With this clearer awareness of the conditions people are operating in, the authors suggest that embodied practitioners possessing increased system awareness are imbued with the power to change their practice and the systems they are operating in.

This book is a tool to use as you work on the challenges you face in your daily practice. With varying levels of granularity, we are introduced to the idea that we are in fact better together. By using what we find in the work we do, and sharing those artifacts with others, we begin to build community capacity for collective action. We are introduced to the idea that research on our practice with others in our community is the heartbeat of informed social action. Through case study vignettes, we see and hear colleagues learning by doing. Those examples are situated in contexts and then used to teach a structure for meeting new challenges. In this way the authors help us learn to hear what is present and what might otherwise remain silent. The sense we get in successive chapters is that there is a way to both increase our curiosity and document our process so others can see what we're doing. The iterative cycle they describe is grounded in gathering evidence and paying attention to how you make meaning of that evidence. We are given a way to observe our mindsets and begin to bring more consciousness to our questions and interpretations.

"Community-Owned Knowledge" is an invitation to bear witness to your individual and collective practice. We are all intertwined and embedded in conditions that are always changing. Seeing these living patterns and giving voice to your experience with others in your community is what this book is about. You'll be encouraged to get as present as you can possibly be with yourself, the evidence, and your community so that more good and greater harmony are possible. The act of learning, and how that learning is measured, is always happening at the intersection of multiple forms of power. The "promise of collaborative action research" resides in its power to help practitioners describe the intersectionality and inter-subjectivity, what some call the situatedness, of actors in a system. With these relationships more clearly described and explicit, the opportunity for agency, to choose transformation or reproduction, is available to everyone.

The authors are asking you to join a coalition of protective agents. Practitioners who belong to a community are committed to finding ways for children and colleagues to share what they know and for them to learn what they need to know. Institutional research has a long history of "othering" the lived experience of people who are not part of white dominant cultural norms. In these pages, you'll meet individuals and communities sharing multiple ways to generate more caring responses, and you'll learn a way to develop an ever-expanding set of liberatory practices. As you open these pages, I encourage you to consider your role in changing systems for good. Connecting with others and sharing your thinking is a powerful act of social change. The "Community-Owned Knowledge" you already have and will continue to create is the foundation of a pluralistic democracy where everyone truly belongs. Learning to share what we know is an important step toward community well-being. I think you'll find this book a useful tool to use on your own and a gift for building meaningful relationships that will sustain you.

*Tony Smith is the co-founder of Whyspeople, providing strategic advising and executive coaching to leaders working to create thriving communities. Most recently Tony served as the Illinois State Superintendent of Education. Prior to serving in that role he was the Executive Director of the W. Clement and Jessie V. Stone Foundation funding early childhood, youth development, and education. He has served in leadership roles in the nonprofit, higher education, and public pk-12 district sectors including Superintendent in the school districts of Emeryville and Oakland, CA. He earned a Ph.D. in Language, Literacy, and Culture from UC Berkeley.

Tony is committed to creating healthy public systems that fully develop the whole child, whole school, and whole community. He measures his work by the increase in fair access to quality, the increase in student and adult belongingness, and the increase in equitable student outcomes that improve economic and civic well-being in the community. He believes that communities working together can deconstruct white supremacy and create new forms of just democracy where all people thrive.

Preface

The onset of the Covid-19 pandemic, which shifted schooling from in-person classes to distance learning modes, coincided with the completion of this book. This moment in our history serves as an exclamation point to emphasize that no existing teacher's manual or education policy handbook could fully prepare teachers, leaders, and administrators for the moment. During this time, we see, through the power of collaborative action, educators exercising their professional responsibilities to provide safe and meaningful educational experiences for their students and taking action to build knowledge as a common good by acting, reflecting, correcting, and then taking action again.

The vision for writing this book came from Gilberto's years of close work with teachers and educational leaders intent on transforming schools and programs for more equitable learning experiences in anti-racist settings that dismantle biased institutional structures. In his work, teams of educational leaders follow action research methods to critically reflect on how they might embed purposeful, collective inquiry into the culture of their schools' work and professional development.

Lyn joined the project after years teaching in public schools and universities. Nearly three decades ago, he and his colleagues undertook CAR before they had a name for the evidenced-based, transformational work that they were undertaking but with a dedication to transforming their school in order to benefit the students' learning outcomes. His focus continues today in preparing teachers and educational leaders with the understandings, habits, and skills of research to promote students' right to build a better future for themselves, their families, and the country.

Together our collaboration within the university and across the college's departments produced this book for those who want to become physically involved as active participants in understanding actions and constructing knowledge in their own schools. To do this, we must follow a process that is deliberate, systematic, and organized. First planning and then implementing the plan one step at a time as teachers, leaders, and administrators working together build our capacity to generate our own knowledge.

Acknowledgments

This book was possible thanks to the ongoing contributions of a committed group of scholar practitioners to the field of education. Their studies have served as inspiration to us, and some of these were cited throughout the book. A few requested to stay anonymous. We list here the names of the scholar practitioners who agreed to have their names public:

    Katelyn La Pine
    Kelly Noriega
    Jennifer Rohrback
    Amy Marymor
    Mirel Rivera
    Kira Walsh
    Yvonne L White
    Elizabeth Brook Garza
    Melissa Reese

Introduction

We subscribe to the idea that research, whether basic or applied, exists to improve life. Thus, we have written this book for teachers, leaders, and administrators interested in transforming their work place, their community, in fact any learning environment. We know that the most effective way individuals, groups, and social networks learn is by simply reflecting critically about their actions. The act of learning typically follows a three-step process: act, reflect, and correct and back to acting again. We conceive this activity as an upward spiral movement. When we come back to acting again, we do so on the bases of the lessons learned. Thus, learning is an open circle that moves up, always one step above the previous one, generating a new cycle at a higher vantage point. Human organizations habituated to a cycle of learning like this one tend to grow, sustain change, and become more democratic and successful at what they do.

This learning process, nonetheless, occurs out of a clear understanding of the value of local knowledge production, and of purposeful and well-organized inquiry efforts, which are all tied to communication. Clarity of values and commitments stems from communication systems that both consistently infuse learning as a shared endeavor and unambiguously embrace inquiry as a means to build knowledge as a common good. A learning and democratized organization does it so intentionally, because it purports to improve all stakeholders' lives.

An organization's purposeful inquiry becomes embedded in the culture until cemented in the institution's edifice. To get to this point, an organization needs to place research on the year's professional development schedule, provide time, and make available material resources and money. It also needs to establish functional data systems and prepare participants with the skills of research—particularly CAR—essential to uncover meanings.

Before moving ahead, let's review what learning itself means and how it happens. In an ideal situation, we learn when we make inferences, predict what may happen, and then explain what happened. In other words, experience naturally leads to understanding. We say it this way because understanding requires deliberate assessment and analysis of an occurrence. That is, we learn when we reflect, and reflection leads to understanding.

As advanced by L. Vygotsky (1962) and A. Leont'ev (1981), no separation exists between our capacity to understand and the physical (whether social, material, cultural) world we are immersed in. We learn by doing. When we participate in an activity, we unleash a series of interactions with the object of said action. We become physically involved as active participants in an action that, in turn, helps shape our thoughts, which at that juncture helps us frame the way we interact with the world. The learning that occurs as a result of our reflective interactions constitutes knowledge when accumulated and kept in our memory.

Attaining knowledge occupies central stage in this book. The accumulated learning used to be passed on from generation to generation through oral traditions. Humanity now counts with quite diverse means—from the printed press to visual, sound, and digital formats. In human organizations, knowledge transmission takes place when the dissemination of knowledge moves on from social group to social group; in other words, as Berger and Luckmann (1966) explained, when the ways to do things in an organization turn into a sediment upon which everyday activities are grounded. At the point when said ways are normalized, it can then be said that knowledge has successfully become institutionalized.

We understand knowledge production as an endeavor that exhibits a set of four essential features. For knowledge to be meaningful to all members of an organization, it grows from the bottom up, inductively, it is rooted on evidence, it must improve life conditions, and it needs to follow a method.

When we say that knowledge grows from the bottom up, we mean that its production stems from the labor of those involved in an action. These actors first reflect on both the action, and its effects on the targeted object; it is them who, from this point, generate the understanding, and over time, the knowledge rendered by the experience of such action. Thus, knowledge originates from lived experiences. Direct and corroborated observation of an action's implementation and its effects make up the evidence that tells us something exists. More in general, any phenomenon that we observe and that others can corroborate forms the core of what constitutes preponderant evidence. If I feel in my head rain drops, and look up the sky and realize that lots of drops are falling, then I may shout: "it's raining!," and if those around me confirm my observation, then we have sufficient evidence that it is raining.

Knowledge, nonetheless, must signify something positive, and beneficial to individuals and to the common good. If we all realize that water falling from the sky can be saved and that way helps us prevent drought during the dry season, so that we all have enough liquid to satiate our thirst, cooking, sanitary, and irrigation needs, we may agree that our knowledge of hydraulics allowed us develop technologies to preserve and adequately use water. Yet, to arrive to this point we embraced a process of knowledge construction.

In order for us to construct knowledge we need to follow a process similar to the one used in erecting a building—deliberate, systematic, and organized. Construction crews start by first having a plan and then implementing it one step at a time: from collecting all the supplies, digging and erecting a foundation, and constructing from here all the parts dictated by the plan. In knowledge production, we first figure the challenge out, ask questions, study the available knowledge, and then map out a plan tracking a purposeful, focused, step-by-step method. As way back as the late sixteenth and early seventeenth centuries Europe, Bacon (1911) had postulated the decisive value of a method, and gave us positivism. He argued that without a method all intelligent effort could easily go to waste. Bacon compared the work of a researcher to that of a bee.

Albeit entomologically inaccurate, Bacon said that a bee takes in the nectar of flowers, process it in its stomach, and then spits it out as honey. The insect transforms the material nature provides, into a completely new product, one that benefits us. The researcher, keeps on explaining, asks a question, and reads on the book of nature for an answer; from the empirical evidence collected, the researcher makes inferences, processes these analytically, and then brings out a new product: knowledge for the betterment of life.

While revolutionary for his time, some of the author's assertions miss fundamental aspects of the human experience, which we tried to address throughout the book. We consider, notwithstanding, core principles: knowledge as a result of induction, knowledge as grounded on evidence, knowledge as a means to improve life conditions, and knowledge as result of method. In addition, we consider three more views: the utility of external support, the indispensable role of leadership, and the significance of networking.

External Support. We understand how complicated it is to look an organization from within. The high degree of intimate involvement in one's institution—whether a school, college, or a non-profit, health organization—inevitably biases and, therefore, might make one's views opaque. The immersion in an organization's daily affairs may be so intense that, like the fish in the water, participants may not be able to discern what is happening. To put it another way, the truth can be so powerful and so close to our eyes that it might blind us. This means that in order to better research our organization, one must walk away some distance and create some detachment from it. Paraphrasing Bakhtin (1992), we can say that to know what surrounds us, we must step outside of it. Yet, when, for whatever reason, it is not possible to distance oneself from the subject of study, bringing in aid from outside may help. External eyes may afford a clearer view, and a more impartial perspective to the issues under our study.

External participation in a localized study can add not only a new, refreshing, and impartial view, but also expertise. In this sense, selecting external support needs to take into account how well informed about the issues being studied these individuals may be, their experience on said issues, and the research technologies they may avail to our institution. When needed, partnering with universities, research centers, and technical assistance non-governmental organizations may be a good way to do this. In addition to external support, inquiry benefits from the direct involvement of the institution's leadership.

Leadership. The quality of the relationship between researcher teams and the organization's governance is key to an inquiry process. We understand that research-based change seeks to ultimately affect an organization's culture, and that change stays made when it sediments and becomes part of the ways things are done. These two assumptions imply that leadership—from top administrators and leaders, to the ground level—must be fully involved to increase our chances of success in our efforts to transform our institution. This collaboration is, therefore, crucially central, for a collaborative and collegial relationship will always be constructively superior to any other, such as adversarial, competitive, or even congenial ones.

Networking. A bottom-up effort, a high-quality external support, and a full collaboration between the leadership and the base take place within networks. A smart organization fosters collaborative research networks where people fully participate in the different steps of the research process, especially defining the challenge and formulating the research questions. These networks assemble inquiry teams organized throughout the organization, and function pretty much like the cells of the human body—reproducing, and infusing energy at all times. They incubate internal capacity to produce local knowledge, making an organization a learning, smart, community; one that fosters ownership of both the inquiry process and the knowledge produced. The denser the leadership and inquiry networks the higher the potential for the know-how, and the sense of collective accomplishment. This assertion, though, assumes that the institution possesses a good degree of stability in its leadership, and the rank and file remain very low. Keeping turnover low helps building capacity.

This book aims at supporting organizations to grow local capacity and improve practice. We have designed six chapters following the logic of the research methodology:

Chapter One. The Concept: Addresses CAR as the larger conceptual framework, and breaks it down into its core components. The chapter also delves into the notions of collaboration, action, and social and cultural capital.

Chapter Two. Identifying the Challenge: Describes the components of a supportive environment, the nature of the challenge, the habits and procedures to define it, and how to situate the challenge and the type of actions. The chapter also discusses the role of culture and structures, evidence, and attribution.

Chapter Three. The Question: Synthesizes the challenge and guides entirely our research. The chapter explains the research question creation process and guides the team's production of a research question. The chapter also operationalizes the research question into its various parts.

Chapter Four. What Is Known and What Is Possible: Provides a systematic and logical way to examine existing knowledge and develop a plan to search databases for research literature. The chapter identifies primary sources of information such as peer-reviewed research articles published in academic journals. The chapter also guides the team in synthesizing information, citing references, and writing the literature review.

Chapter Five. The Method: Explains how to conduct qualitative research. The chapter defines qualitative methodology as highly adaptive and inductive. It also delves with data collection rigor and bias control. The chapter also explains the functions of population and sampling, and data collection strategies.

Chapter Six. The Analysis: Focuses on data reduction and data display. The chapter describes four core concepts of data analysis. It explains the typical steps to break data down into meaningful pieces for analytical purposes. The chapter shows six different ways to display data and closes with templates for reporting results.

References

Bacon, F. (1911). *The novum organum.* New York, NY: P.F. Collier and Son. Facsimile by Library Services of Ball State University, Muncie, IN.

Bakhtin, M. M. (1992). *The dialogic imagination. Four essays.* Austin, TX: University of Texas Press.

Berger, P. L., & Luckmann, T. (1966). *The social construction of reality. A treatise in the sociology of knowledge.* Garden City, NY: Anchor Books.

Leont'ev, A. N. (1981). *Problems of the development of mind.* Moscow: Progress Publishers.

Vygotsky, L. S. (1962). *Thought and language.* Cambridge, MA: M. I. T. Press, and New York, NY: John Wiley and Sons, Inc.

1 The Concept

Yearly, Argot High teachers fill out a Google form with recommendations for what classes students should take next year. I became close with a group of students who were in my first period class. I also had some of them for a second period in a support class called "Integrated Algebra 3–4". I found out about the struggles many of these students' families were facing. For instance, a student's dad had lost his job and lost their house as well. The family had to move in with his sister and brother-in-law. I learned about many similar situations others are dealing with on a daily basis.

I recommended these students to take Algebra II the following year, because I strongly believed they had the tools to be successful in the next level math class. The support class was eliminated but as a department it was decided to create a new one called "Algebra II light". In essence it was the same support class I had worked on, which the department had just canceled. Some of the students facing these family problems were placed into the new support class, instead of the regular Algebra II, even when their grades and my recommendations showed they could take it.

I didn't find out about the changes until a couple of weeks after and nothing could be done at that point since all regular Algebra II classes were full. I felt frustrated about the changes, and believed we weren't equitable with these students; besides, this kind of action has happened more than once in the last couple of years. Fortunately, a few of my students recommended for the support class were given the spots in the regular Algebra II class, but only after their parents pushed for the change and signed a waiver.

> We are a unified district, and within our boundaries we take any student along with the disadvantages that may come with them. Argent High prides itself in being the most academic campus in the district and I can attest to that. However, by looking at academic data, I have learned we have a large group of students who are suffering of the injustices of living in the changing economic conditions of our geographical area. We've had many students whose families had to move out, because they cannot afford to live in the city they grew up in, or they have stayed in but have struggled to make ends meet. There is much work that we can do and need to be done if we believe all students can learn.
>
> Rafael Mora. (notes from "Defining the Problem." March, 2018)

Rafael Mora tells us an ongoing story of a challenge teachers frequently face, or witness at their sites. Too many incidents of this kind constantly occur, to the point that to redress each one of them in real time may simply not be possible. But then inevitable moments like the one he described linger and force teachers to do something right away. Nevertheless, confronted by the same situation some may become passively cynical, but most, like Mr. Mora, will very likely act.

When a situation like the one he describes occurs in front of us, the action that comes next may determine the fate of many. To act, "Mr. M," as youngsters and adults call him at the school, will probably draw on a repertoire of skills and understanding of the issue at hand, which he has accumulated over years of service. Cognizant of the urgency to repair the challenges facing students, he will immediately sort out two possible reactions—(a) aid the students in the moment, and (b) do something to deal with the issue at a deeper, long-term level. For the former, he knows he ought to immediately engage his academic department's colleagues and the school's administrators, so that to find an immediate remedy. For the latter, though, Mr. M. will very likely rely on an inquiry process that involves other colleagues, and follows an action research cycle.

In the next sections of this chapter, we explain each of the three central components of CAR. We start with the "R": the nature of research, then we delve into the "C": the value of collaboration, and close with the "A": the role of action as generator of social and cultural capital.

Nature of Collaborative Action Research

Action research is perhaps the most applied of all existing research approaches. Whether people call it this way or not, inquiry embedded in action is a type of action research. What makes *action research* different from, say, survey designs, is its *solving*-oriented nature, which takes a five-step sequence: identification of a challenge, intentional implementation of an action (also called the intervention), research the results of the intervention (examine whether the governing variables have changed), learn from experience, make any needed modification, and then go back again to initiate a new cycle.

Action research, we believe, traces its origins to the very existence of our species. By definition, we always wonder the "if" of things, as in "what would happen if I do this?" Through millennia that very wondering has steered us to discovery and invention. Our quest for knowledge has afforded great benefits—from the discovery of fire and cooking, to agriculture and the formation of the homo sapiens' permanent settlements, germs theory and antibiotics, to astrophysics, digital technology, artificial intelligence, and nanotechnology.

As a formal methodological approach, though, action research goes back only a few decades in the United States. K. Lewin seems to have been the first to have argued for its importance in an article published in 1946 entitled "Action Research and Minority Problems." The MIT Professor argues that to address intergroup conflict in a manner that helps the country to become a more integrated society, a different type of research was needed:

> The research needed for social practice can best be characterized as research for social management, or social engineering. It is a type of action-research, a comparative research on the conditions and effects of various forms of social action, and research leading to social action. Research that produces nothing but books will not suffice. (p. 35)

Lewin continues arguing that a research approach of this kind would be as scientific, if not more, as any other of the recognized approaches.

However, action research had been practiced throughout the country for decades. Myles Horton, for example, founded in 1932 the Highlanders Folk School, in the Appalachia region, based on the principles of action research and popular education. The school dedicated its efforts to improving the living conditions of rural and urban communities by educating civic and community organizers. It played a key role during the civil rights movement, where activists, such as Rosa Parks, honed their political and activist skills.

Collaboration was not originally part of the approach. Paulo Freire—whose work "Education as a practice of freedom" in 1966, synthesized his literacy experiences of late 1950s and early 1960s in Brazil and Chile—championed collaboration as a core component of action research. He used the term "participatory action research."

Participatory and collaborative to us mean the same. His literacy approach equipped impoverished rural communities in those countries to investigate their own condition, and helped galvanize their collective action to change their life circumstances.

Core Components

Collaborative action research—heretofore also identified as CAR—besides collaboration, brings to the process of action research a few extra steps that strengthens the rigor of research, which we explain in the next chapters of this book:

(a) Identifying the challenge also entails formulating a research question, or set of core questions, to anchor the investigation. This is the content of Chapter Three.
(b) Searching for solutions to the challenge means studying the available knowledge about previous studies and experiences with both the challenge and the solutions. This is the content of Chapter Four.
(c) Implementing a solution implies a parallel and methodical study of its effects. The careful selection of a method may determine the success of the entire process. This is the content of Chapter Five.
(d) Learning and making modifications only happens if the process we followed carefully and systematically analyzes and presents the results in a rigorous manner. This is the content of Chapter Six.

Figure 1.1: Five steps of collaborative action research
Source: G. Arriaza © 2020

Whether a school, a college, a hospital, a construction company, a neighborhood, or a town, CAR is a methodological framework grounded on concrete and pressing needs of an organization. It is a reiterative, collaborative, adaptable, and inferential approach that contains an action. Generally speaking, the methodology moves in a four-lane track, like a wide, one-way road.

One lane, *the iterative side*, runs through a process akin to that of an upward spiral: a cycle ends when it comes back to its point of departure. But when it does, it comes back to a higher vantage point. This assertion assumes that inquiry may have unearthed new knowledge, and new understandings that make the groove of the new cycle to move up. The new cycle starting at the end of the previous one may show a change in the direction of improvement, may push the inquiry back to refine its own assumptions, redefine the question, or even start anew from the definition of the problem. Either way, there is no going back to the original conditions that prompted the inquiry in the first place. This iteration encompasses a study's full cycle.

The iterations also occur at every step of a cycle. Research teams continuously examine the collected data against the methodology and the study's goals. This comparative process occurs via consultations between the principal research team and the rest of the organization. They will recalibrate the research process when issues are revealed by this comparative process. The frequent checking-in also contributes to trust building among all members of the organization.

These momentary pauses may stimulate support and build will, and over the long haul, may contribute to growing learning communities, and to deepening a sense of collective ownership of knowledge production.

The second lane, *the collaborative side*, moves in starts and halts. Research teams go back to the larger constituency to share data, study results, and methodological challenges. They look for input, advice, more evidence, and insights to improve the inquiry project, modify procedures, and discuss the content, and the key feature of the design is to implement any warranted changes on practice—like climbing a tree while studying the health status of its bark.

The third lane, *the adaptability nature of the approach*, infuses great flexibility to research. Fitting the design to the challenge and its evolution is an unrelenting research necessity. As the tracks of a train trace topography's bends, the straight lines of valleys, and every hill's ups and downs, CAR follows the empirical reality. Adaptability here means that as content may shift, the procedures may need to also change. Having a great deal of methodological flexibility is crucial. Action research design provides such adaptability—it always matches the nature of the problem.

12 | *Community-Owned Knowledge*

The fourth lane *grounds the entire approach on a bottom-up mode.* Action research is an inferential approach in that it is originated and sustained by the evidence collected. Preconceived assumptions and theories are left on the side. The approach builds from participants' lived experience within the institution where the study takes place. In fact, the organization pulses through them. Hence, as members of the organization researchers enjoy great access to the evidence at all times, which, in turn, avails them a continuous exchange with the sources. This way, researchers can establish a constant checking in between what reality tells, and what the collected data indicate.

See the four components in Figure 1.2.

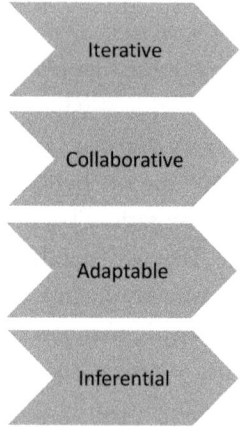

Figure 1.2: The four lanes of collaborative action research methodology
Source: G. Arriaza © 2020

An important caveat about the latter feature: digging deep into one's own environment makes it hard to infer refreshing and new truths. Whereas the research team's immersion in the organization's life world allows members to hold great expertise on the subject matter—they know their organizations as no external researchers ever could—it also represents perhaps the greatest risk—bias.

We all know how bias coils deep in our consciousness, ready to spring at any time. As researchers we cannot ignore, nor afford acting on them. Doing so would render useless any understanding emerging from our research work. But, here we offer three ways to keep tabs on bias:

(a) Collaborative action research's iterative checking between research teams and the rest of the organization must definitely help. The going back-and-forth between sharing the collected data and having a sense how the rest of our coworkers react and engage these data, makes it possible to establish the necessary distance one needs to critically look back onto one's work.

Let's emphasize: constant checking in is a deliberate mechanism that helps us stay honest.
(b) The purpose of CAR is to apply the newly discovered understandings. The notion that we seek better and clearer understandings of a challenge to transform life circumstances is what anchors CAR. That is, we study with the purpose of redressing inequities and injustices. We simply mean that we do not pursue, as our primary concern, the creation of theory. This premise suggests that we take on the evidence we have collected, and then we analyze, and interpret it without trying to make it fit a given theoretical framework.

c) The collaborative nature of action research builds in a habit of checks and balances. It indeed offers us a uniquely strong opportunity to control individual and collective proclivities when collecting, analyzing, and especially, interpreting the evidence. Collaborating makes us, individually, accountable to the collective, and likewise, the collective accountable to the individual members of the team. Openly transparent collaboration makes us more authentic and open-minded.

These dynamics—the individual and the group, and the group and the individual—raise another core issue: who jumps into action and what spaces exist for the enactment of change.

Agency and Agents

Margaret Mead's frequently cited and catchy statement illustrates our understanding of the meaning of agency and agents:

> Never doubt that a small group of thoughtful, committed citizens can change the world; indeed, it's the only thing that ever has.

CAR happens when and only if individuals take on the responsibility to act when they know, as Mr. Mora from the story at the beginning of this chapter does, that something is not right. Mr. Mora knows that he has to act immediately by asking his department to redress the immediate situation. That is active, engaged agency. But then, Mr. Mora also knows that to find a sustainable, long-term solution to the challenge, he ought to initiate an action research cycle to investigate the challenge at the root level. That is strategic agency.

In our model, all members of an organization can participate as principal researchers or as support. They all can exert agency and, thus, be agents of knowledge production and transformative change. In other words, each member of an organization embodies agency.

Agency constitutes the possibility of acting to address an issue and solve a challenge.

Agency is always present, like compressed energy at the ready. In physics this is called potential energy. In action research, agency lives in all of us, the would-be agents. It transcends easily individual self-interest, and work for the organization as a whole, for the common good. Yet, not always all members of an organization become agents, and agents do not necessarily act all the times. Agents may possess sets of skills, habits, understanding, and knowledge that, at a minimum, predispose them to dealing with the organization's vexing issues.

An agent purposefully dedicates time, and labor to improve the organization, so that to keep it oriented toward its objectives and goals; in other words, delivering its promised benefits to the end consumers of the goods and services created by it. End consumers, in a school context, centrally include students, and through them their families. School staff and the school's surrounding community, albeit indirectly, also gain from the results.

Agents work in teams, sometimes called professional learning communities, communities of practice, and intervention committees. For the purposes of this book, we call them Principal Research Teams and Support Research Teams. We detail these teams later in this chapter. Nevertheless, and regardless the name, at the center of these learning communities sit inquiry, more concretely, collaborative action research. Tied to the organization's professional development plans, these learning communities enjoy allocated time and are listed on the official calendar.

Informal learning communities also exist, and agents play crucial roles in their formation and operations. But informal learning communities' agency must percolate the organization's formal functioning. Here is why this is so necessary: as long as the agency of informal learning communities does not attach their action to the formal operations of an organization, and the leadership does not recognize and respect it, they risk marginalization and, over the long haul, irrelevance. We believe that for change to stay made, it must become part of the institution. That is, instituted in such a way that members of the organization incorporate change into their daily routines, to the point that these become normalized. This is what true transformative change means.

The Value of Collaboration

People researching together very likely will own the process and its results together. In the sections above, we have asserted that collaboration helps us to be more honest and authentic. In this section, we place collaboration within its social context and locate the role of practice at the core of it. Thus, we detail how to grow collaborative research from groups to teams, and their networking dynamics.

Collaboration Is Socially Situated

First things first: Let's revisit some foundational norms.

Action research occurs in terms of social relations, and it is situated within concrete spaces. Even though the tendency to isolate oneself seems ever present, individuals working in an institution always depend on each other. Typically, teachers talk to each other in shared spaces, such as the halls and the copy and resources rooms; when this happens the talk not necessarily is oriented to dealing with the challenges that practice may raise, nor these contacts always forge deeper relationships, commitments, and learning opportunities.

Too frequently, parking lot encounters only lead to the exchange of snippets of information and surface-level social relations. People forge communities when sharing a common purpose, through concrete acts linked to their environment.

Collaborative inquiry offers a venue to end fragmented relationships. It also promotes conversation with a focus on practice. Certainly, the most effective and enriching inquiry always originates from a shared concern about the possible reasons something exists, and how we do the things we do. When these concerns emerge from the base—classroom teachers, for instance—and become part of an ever-wider conversation, we say that we have created a bottom-up inquiry.

Nevertheless, inquiries, with the most potent force to enact transformative changes, are the ones raised from the bottom, meeting the administrative leadership's own. Or bottom-up inquiries, powerfully persuasive enough to move the top administrative leadership to embrace them.

Example:
A team of four high school teachers from Los Huertos High, a large, comprehensive semi-rural school noticed that at lunchtime there were two lines of students at the cafeteria's cashier area. Students in one of the lines were showing a red card to pay their meal; the others were showing a blue one. Red meant discounted lunch, blue full pay. Contrary to expectations, the red card holding line was considerably shorter than the other. The school served a majority economically poor population, and considered a Title 1. After consistently tallying the number of adolescents lining up on both lines for a full two weeks, and randomly interviewing them, the research team produced a report on the issue and presented it to the administration's team: low use of the free and reduced lunch program due mostly to stigma.

The research team was gladly surprised to find receptive ears from the very first meeting on. The school's administrators had also been wondering about the same thing, except they didn't have the data from the lunch lines. As a result of various meetings, both teams devised a process to bring the issue to the entire school, from here they planned an action research that included: more fully documenting the issue, piloting an initial solution, and collecting data on the results. The action consisted of the use of an inclusive tracking: a one-color-only card, with funds already allocated for those in the free and reduced lunch program.

Principal and Support Teams

Authors such as Jonassen & Rohrer-Murphy (1999) have noted that the collaborative component of action research implies the participation of teams who contribute to the inquiry effort in myriad of ways. Yet, team formation is more complicated than it sounds. Individuals come typically together to talk about a concern. They will probably decide to work together when realize that they share the same concern, and have the will to do something about it. But they do not form a team yet. For a group to evolve into a team it requires effort, time, and labor.

A look at Tuckman's (1965) group developmental model may be helpful here.

According to the author, a group does become a team after an entire process of socializing. This socialization process occurs through engaged work. Tuckman's model explains this process as a series of four stages. We formatted these stages as a four-step ladder, with the model's first stage at the base.

Performing, the highest stage, here the group's functioning as a team has arrived, where making decisions collaboratively organizes the work, troubleshooting challenges as a team occurs naturally.

Norming, the third stage, which consists of a group's conforming moment to internally facilitated leadership; members have become clearer about ways to find solutions to tasks, and working together.

Storming, the second stage, which consists of a group's emergent moment, where leadership begins to flow from within, and group members begin to embrace the tasks, ideas, and mission as theirs.

Forming, the first stage, consists of the more tentative moment of individuals coming together to perform a task, where external leadership is exerted more directly; also they initially embrace the tasks and mission (see Figure 1.3).

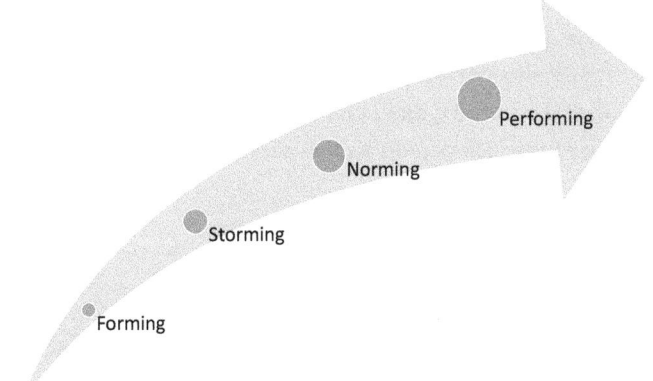

Figure 1.3: Group development model
Source: G. Arriaza © 2020

Members of a team can always change, and when this happens, a team may enter periods of re-acculturation. In other words, new members are brought in while at the same time are intentionally socialized around the team's working habits, norms, and procedures. Thus, the team may be at the performing level, but it may go back to a norming mode to accommodate the newly arrived members. The norming stage may, therefore, be visualized as a continuum toward performing, and not as an end in itself.

18 | *Community-Owned Knowledge*

Teams, over time, will necessarily grow into different stages of maturity but not in a strict linear fashion. Depending on how participatory the organization's culture may be, teams and the institution's leadership distribute and take on tasks and responsibilities throughout the central steps of the inquiry.

We consider at least two kinds of teams: principal research teams—who work together leading and orchestrating the entire enterprise—and support research teams, who contribute to this endeavor. We conceive this collaboration as a multiple and dynamic social web, where at the center we locate the principal research team, who exhibit the curiosity, skills, and determination to initiate the inquiry conversation.

Next to the principal research team, we find sets of teams or groups of individuals who immediately embark on the same talk, but who are not conducting the research; and then yet another set of teams or groups, less interested, but willing to eventually engage in the conversation, and who sit more in the periphery of a particular study.

At the edge of these teams and groups remain all other members of the organization, including non-teaching staff—such as custodians and other school services personnel—who not merely observe the activities; they eventually will become involved as the inquiry moves forward and somehow touches their interest. The following Figure 1.4 depicts a cross section of this social web.

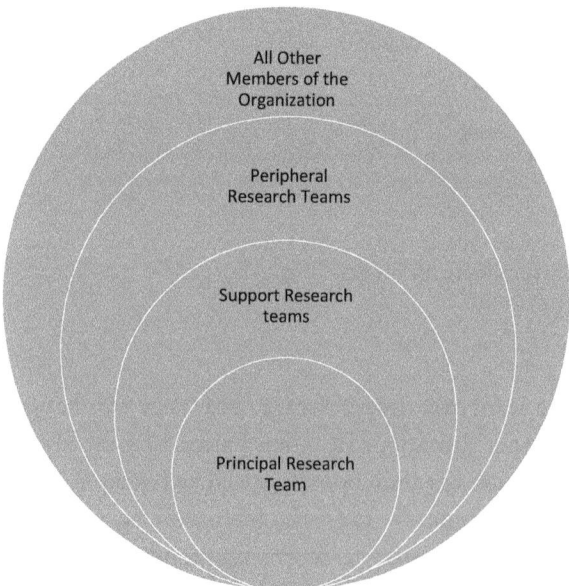

Figure 1.4: Social web
Source: G. Arriaza © 2020

Again, at the core of the web resides the principal research team, and all the existing social webs gyrate around conversations on a particular study stimulated by this team, and its closest collaborators. We need to keep in mind the phrase "a particular study," because there might be a few other studies happening simultaneously. So, it is very possible that a team that may be supported, or peripheral in a particular study's conversation, could actually be the principal research team of another study.

In a human organization, the more the overlapping and multi-functions of groups' and teams' inquiry work occur, the denser, diverse, and resilient its research culture is. This multi-layered inquiry life indeed nurtures leadership and local knowledge production, and raises the organization's collective capacity. Just as in nature's ecosystems: the more diverse and dense the healthier they become.

Collaboration has marked humanity's historical experience. Collaborating made it possible for the Homo sapiens to survive through millennia when competing against predators and other species to establish and, eventually, control territory. As Maturana & Varela (1987) and Gould (1996) have argued, beginning with our own body systems, we function on the basis of absolute collaboration. In a study on memory, Kandel in 2007 explains how our brain's neuronal networks transmit their signals in simultaneous coordination from network to network; these networks learn how to cooperate among themselves by repeating their interactions continuously, until they "wire together."

Individualism and competition are both the opposite to the ways our bodies work. In spite of the emphasis contemporary societies made on individualism, which appears strong and signals a behavior that tends to rather fracture society, we have no option but to work together primarily due to the interdependent nature of the globalized economy and to an increasingly contracted planet. We are in this together.

Collaboration within and across Disciplines

Ms LaPine, Ms Noriega, and Ms Rohrbach, a research team from the LaCroix Unified School District, articulated collaboration this way: "[Collaborative action research] is a vehicle to a more democratic institution that makes site based decisions on the voices of the many rather than the few." As these researchers noted, the collective nature of the research process not only opens the opportunity to a multiplicity of voices but also opens the process to multiple disciplines perspectives. We can bring these disciplines either as separate, one-dimensional layer, called intradisciplinary; or as a set of discreet, separate analytical layers, called interdisciplinary, or we can bring these disciplinary layers integrated into one analytical tool, called transdisciplinary. They all will aid our efforts to bring into clearer view the issue we are researching.

A visual metaphor may help here. When we do analyze an issue, we bring it into focus through our glasses. Intradisciplinary implies our use of one-graduation only pair of glasses. Interdisciplinary refers to the use of a set of separate glasses, each with a different graduation. Transdisciplinary means that we use one multifocal pair of glasses. In optometry, the latter are known as progressive lenses, which adjust the graduation according to the light and distance from an object, correcting nearsighted and farsighted vision.

Disciplinary analysis and collaboration are conjoined dimensions in an organization's inquiry work.

Disciplinary analysis can happen horizontally when people from the same discipline work together to address a common issue. Collaboration in this case is intradisciplinary, for instance, all nine grade English language teachers studying social interaction of dual language learners. In this case, the effort is three-way horizontal—same grade (9th), same discipline (English), and same common issue (social interactions).

In addition, the same case but with a variation: instead of only one grade level, the disciplinary analysis is being done across the four high school grade levels. In this case, the study still is intradisciplinary since it is studying the issue from the same discipline (English), and same common issue (social interaction). But the collaboration contains a vertical dimension—9th, 10th, 11th, and 12th grades.

Disciplinary analysis can also happen horizontally when people from different disciplines work together to solve a common issue. Collaboration here is interdisciplinary: for instance, teachers from mathematics, chemistry, earth sciences, and history addressing academic literacy among native English speakers in the ninth grade only. In this case, the effort is three-way horizontal—same grade level (9th), same common issue (academic literacy), and same grade level from multiple disciplines (math, chemistry, earth sciences, and history).

As in the social interaction case, in the academic literacy, instead of only one grade level, the collaboration is being done across the four high school grade levels. In this case the study still is interdisciplinary. It is horizontal in the sense that it is looking at the same common issue (academic literacy), but with a vertical interdisciplinary twist, (a) it is following a collaboration from multiple disciplines (math, chemistry, earth sciences, and history), but (b) the collaboration involves now 9th, 10th, 11th, and 12th grade teachers.

Intradisciplinary analysis, again, provides the analytical perspective of one discipline. In our case above the study of social interaction of dual language learners is being designed and will be executed by a team of English language teachers. They will very likely follow sociolinguistics as the lens, and probably bring into their CAR methodological approaches from said discipline.

When the LaCroix School District team was designing the study on homework completion, the three members looked at the issue from a social communications perspective. The three-team members counted on their social science backgrounds to do this work. Might there have been a team member with a background on economics, they could have probably added a perspective on the income structure of the participating students' families, including their neighborhood's housing, employment, local businesses, and other relevant economic indicators. Then the study would have been interdisciplinary. But it was not.

Interdisciplinary analysis brings to the fore different angles to examine the issue of academic literacy, whether the study design and execution is limited to one school grade level or many school grade levels. As in the academic literacy case, the participants from the different disciplines (math, chemistry, earth sciences, and history) come with their discipline background, and besides their particular analytical perspective, they bring a diverse research approach to the CAR project.

Intra- and interdisciplinary collaboration offer different benefits and limitations to the labor of knowledge creation for an institution. Intradisciplinary studies make it possible to zero in on concrete issues bounded by a scientific discipline. Its sharp focus may allow to go deeper into potential factors governing the issue being studied, but the unidimensional nature of intradisciplinary inquiry may set up boundaries that may not allow to see beyond into many other factors influencing the issue. The analysis that emerges from this approach might be deep and narrow at the same time. The LaCroix School District case above may help here as illustration.

Following a social communication frame analysis, the study conducted at the LaCroix by La Pine, Noriega, and Rohrbach looked at low homework completion rates among their students in social studies. The team designed a controlled, very precise communication interaction data collection plan. They hypothesized that personal phone calls to parents (as opposed to making home visits, sending electronic notes, and mailing formal letters) would be a good behavior modifier. While the collaboration included three different schools, the study was intradisciplinary. Figure 1.5 illustrates this point.

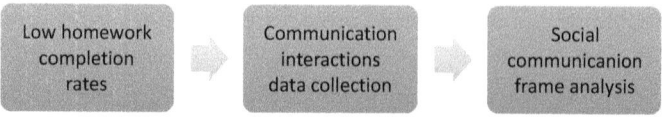

Figure 1.5: Intradisciplinary
Source: G. Arriaza © 2020

On the other hand, interdisciplinary studies may widen the scope of knowledge creation. For instance, the same La Pine, et al. study on low homework completion rates could have enriched the analysis, if each of the three researchers had examined the issue from at least three positions:

(a) The impact of personalized phone calls to parents, from the perspective of cross-cultural communication.
(b) The nature of power interactions between parents and teachers from social reproduction theory.
(c) The content of narrative patterns from parents' verbal responses.

These three disciplines could have enriched the understanding of the issue in ways that only one perspective could have not. Moreover, the three disciplines could have brought in diverse methodological approaches to the study, such as critical discourse analysis. Figure 1.6 illustrates this case.

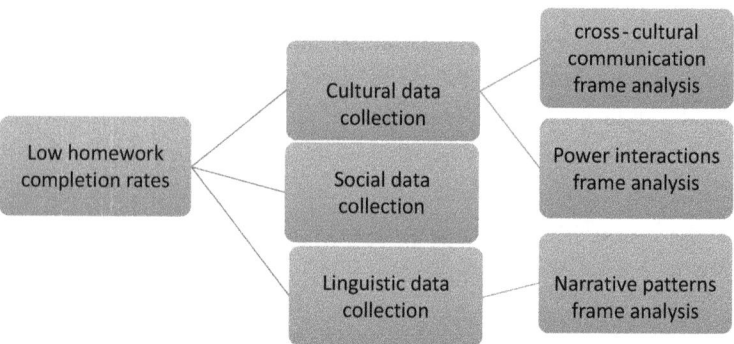

Figure 1.6: Interdisciplinary
Source: G. Arriaza © 2020

While interdisciplinary studies bring complex and layered perspectives to a study, transdisciplinary analysis blends these disciplines. Instead of separating the different disciplinary analysis, we bring them together, just as our neuronal networks do: integration and not compartmentalization.

Transdisciplinary analysis makes it possible to illuminate the emerging multiplicity of meanings from the data. This approach starts from the very first step of an inquiry—the definition of the issue. Each of us arrives to the study of a challenge loaded with the theories provided by the scientific background we have been embraced plus all other theoretical baggage we have been espoused or have been exposed to in our life. For purposes of clarity, we include here a diagram showing, from left to right, first the issue being studied; second, data collection following pre-established protocols by field. Third, for purposes of analysis, these data are arranged by organizing all the sets by field; fourth, the analysis phase where all the fields converge as a blended process (see Figure 1.7).

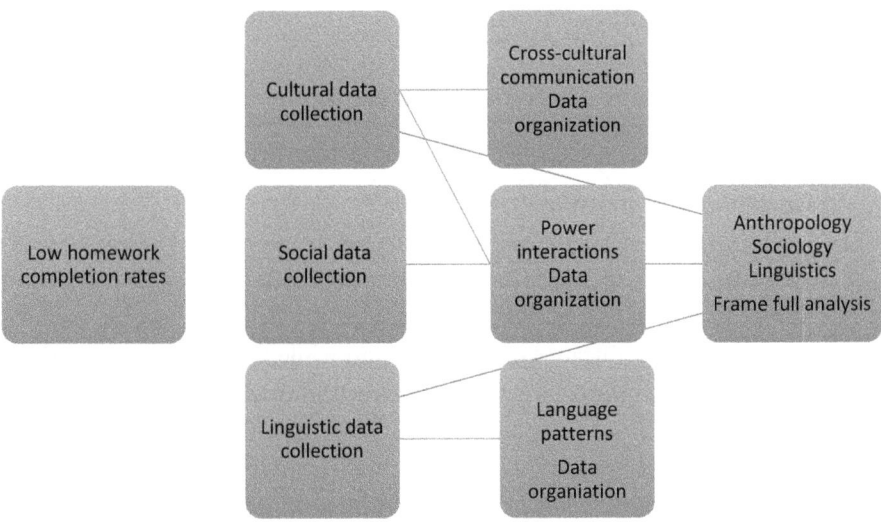

Figure 1.7: Transdisciplinary
Source: G. Arriaza © 2020

We have thus far explained the "R" and the "C" of the triad Collaborative Action Research. We addressed the central aspects of research, and elaborated on the four features of this approach, its bias risk, and how to control it. We showed how knowledge production depends on agents, groups, and teams, and how these agents build smart, learning communities. We delved on collaboration as fundamental bases of an evidence-oriented organizational culture. Collaboration occurs within social relations. The density of these may enhance cohesiveness in organizations, which, in turn, significantly may shrink social distance.

In the next section we focus on the "A" feature of collaborative action research. We show here how the act of social connectivity encompasses the sharing of information, skills, knowledge, traits, and traditions. This sharing undoubtedly adds social and cultural value to the network. Action, in our approach, contains the possibility to serve as conduit to generate capital—social and cultural—for both the research collaboration teams, and the entire organization.

Action and Social and Cultural Capital

Action

First let's talk about the types of action and the link between action with social and cultural capital formation.

CAR involves concrete, laser-focused targeted actions. We distinguish them into two types:

1. Creating a new action

   These actions refer to those situations where a principal research team identifies a challenge, studies it, and finds out that the organization, say a school as a whole, has not taken any action. Typically, individuals are convinced of the significance of the issue, and while the case may have posed a serious challenge over time, no experience addressing it exists at the site. Example:

   First, the three teachers' team from LaCroix Unified School District, which we have mentioned in the previous sections, worked across three different schools (two high schools and one elementary). The team realized that students from low socioeconomic background were consistently showing low rates of homework completion.

   Second, the team considered such rates unacceptable, and conjectured that a relationship between homework completion and low social science academic performance existed.

   Third, the team found no background existed about how the schools or the district had addressed the challenge in the past.

   Fourth, the team decided to affect homework completion, after careful examination of the possible factors underpinning the challenge, by targeting parents. The team formulated this theory of action: *if* parents at home oversee homework, *then* completion will increase *so that*, eventually, students' academic performance in social science might improve.

Fifth, the team was now ready to work on an action plan. They asked this concrete question to guide their action research: To what extent can weekly parent-teacher communication affect homework completion among underserved students?

Sixth, they created a daily scripted call asking parents to supervise their children's work. The first phase took daily calls for a total of six weeks. These six actions made up the first cycle of the inquiry.

Seventh, after collecting data documenting the results, the team studied the degree of homework completion among student participants, examined whether academic results improved.

Eighth, the team then made all necessary adjustments to the action to initiate a new cycle of communication.

2. Interrogating an on-going action

    These actions have been agreed and, in most cases, implemented. While this kind of inquiry may have some evaluative element, it is not an evaluation. The procedure involves a thorough data collection to examine what is being done to address a specific challenge, a rigorous analysis of the data against the action's goals and objectives and, at specific points of the study, the inquiry's findings will inform the action. This feedback loop at times does not exist because of these interventions' contractual limitations. In these cases, the end of an inquiry cycle might mean termination or, if found positive results, the continuation of the intervention.

    Example:

    First, after studying math test scores, a high school principal research team of teachers from the Green Hills Union High School district wanted to understand whether an After School Focused Excellence (SAFE) math program was helping a group of students in the lower quartiles in intermediate algebra.

    Second, the team examined SAFE's reports on the students serviced and the results of a pre- and post-academic test. As these data showed, the program appeared to be having positive results.

    Third, the team hypothesized that the program may have shown great initial results due, in part, to the use of aggregated data of low- and high-performing groups.

Fourth, the team started its own study by surveying all participants (teachers and students) in the SAFE program. The survey included socially and culturally equivalent student groups but performing one at a low, and the other at a high academic levels prior to enrolling in the SAFE program.

Fifth, the team focused on student's perceptions of the program's tutorial services, and whether assiduously attending class impacted academic performance.

Sixth, from the survey the team found out that attendance was inconsistent and low.

Seventh, based on the finding the team decided to add an action piece to their study: sending daily electronic reminders to students to go to the SAFE tutorials.

Eighth, within two weeks, the team saw initial improvements in attendance, and higher quiz scores for the low-performing group.

Ninth, the principal research team did not claim that even a correlation existed between the electronic reminders and improved attendance. Needless to say, they did not argue that attendance improved quiz scores. Yet, both improved attendance and increased quiz scores, indicated that the study's action appeared oriented in the right direction. While this initial results may signal the existence of factors that may require further exploration, the team stayed with the original plan by refining communication with the students to make attendance more reliable.

In the next section, we explore the relationship between CAR with social and cultural capital.

Social and Cultural Capital

We dig deep into the possible root-level factors (also called "governing variables") of a problem we consider a challenge, in order to redress inequities and injustices in our organizations; stated differently, we conduct research to improve life circumstances. As in medicine, scientists search to solve the mysteries of disease, thus reducing the number of deaths, in education we seek to affect the variables that produce a concrete inequity, or an unjust situation, so that to improve students' futures. The findings and the sense-making work we engage in action research ultimately attempt to create higher degrees of understanding, as well as strengthen local capacity to redress such inequities and injustices. Intentionally forging a social and cultural type of capital is the ultimate purpose of collaborative action research.

Before moving on to discuss these two fundamental concepts—social capital and cultural capital—we first must define what capital means in this context. In general, in economic terms, capital means money and material possessions one person or an organization possesses. Money holds several functions. One can convert one form of capital for another; for instance, selling a car for cash. One can also accumulate capital; for instance, saving a portion of a salary in an interests bearing account. One can transfer capital; for instance, wiring money from one account to another. One can exchange capital; for instance, paying a dentist for a filling. One can transport capital from place to place; for instance, bills, credit cards, or a chip, which symbolize money and that one uses in most places at a planetary scale.

Capital also generates more capital when one puts it to work. Capital is linked to productivity. In a capitalist economy, to produce we need the input materials, the necessary labor force, and money capital to lubricate the production machinery. In other words, embedded in the significance of money is its potential to produce more value.

Now, when we say social capital we mean that there exists value, therefore capital, in our relationships. We function in the world in terms of social networks such as family kinship, friendship groups, neighborhood connections, and other smaller social units like a hamlet where everybody knows everybody. Trust, reciprocity, common spaces, shared purposes conform to the core of social capital.

For instance, Christie Rocha and one of us, Gilberto, published a study carried out in a small, K-8 school district that followed a group of classroom teachers. The researchers were concerned with the ways these teachers facilitated the inhibition or creation of social capital among their students. The study "growing social capital in the classroom" published in 2016 found that teachers, while not cognizant of the term, most definitely engaged in daily activities that engendered social capital formation. The study showed how teachers encouraged collective use of classroom supplies, whether these originated at the site or brought from home by the students. In the latter case, teachers requested uniformity for all items, so that more resourceful children would not bring luxurious ones. The resulting sense of reciprocity and collective ownership, the study observed, laid the ground for trust—a foundational component of social networks.

Additionally, the study uncovered that setting classroom expectations, and the habituation of listening activities (through children's out-loud readings, telling personal background stories, speaking in front of the whole class, and working groups), stimulated children's budding friendships, and strengthen existing ones.

The study also sought to explain how the networking taking place in the classroom translated into larger network formations and into the neighborhood. The authors did realize that the classroom networks dissolved in the schoolyard during recession, or lunch break. Instead, most children gravitated toward familiar friendship groups forged in years past. Moreover, while in the classroom children from varied social strata established close connections, once out of the school premises they fragmented mostly by household. Parents appear to not necessarily cultivate new parental friendships, nor to follow the ones their children had just initiated.

The two principal researchers and the support researcher team in this study went through a collective learning. All participants, including among them the school principal, went through a learning experience that translated into deeper understandings of the issues involved. In other words, being aware of the importance of activities as mundane and specific as one's classroom day-to-day schedule aided these educators to be more intentional and explicit, for example, asking children to map out their parents' place of origin, and then telling the story how they ended up living in their current neighborhoods. They also could now frame these activities more explicitly as efforts to grow social capital. The participating principal learned the potential value of all those activities (including children and teachers deciding behavioral norms in the classroom) not simply for management purposes, but as the purposeful effort to unleash the inherent value of social networks, and to forge, in the school premises, a common good.

Cultural capital is distinctively different to social capital. A core idea in cultural capital, which Pierre Bourdieu (1986) coined, is habitus. According to the author, it means the ways we speak, walk, dress, think, and express emotion. Habitus mediates our position in society in terms of social class. In capitalist societies like ours, economic background marks our habitus. Dumais (2005) describes habitus as "attitudes, references, formal knowledge, behaviors" (p. 84) that prevails in society's centers of power. According to Apple (2004) and Delpit (1988), the dominant habitus is that of the economic elites, which schools use to stratify students.

More concretely, we follow here Tramonte and Willms' (2010) notion of static and relational cultural capital. Static cultural capital implies access to established spheres of a dominant culture such as the opera house, the symphony, theater, art museums, and any upper class iconic cultural expressions. Relational cultural capital, on the other hand, means access to cultural knowledge through social contact, starting with children's day-to-day home experience around conversation on politics, the economy, history, moral, and ethical beliefs and behaviors, among others. Deliberately exposing students to both static and relational cultural capital, so that to close the opportunity differential between privileged and disadvantaged students, is part of teacher's role as institutional protective agents.

Institutional protective agents refer to individuals who hold a position of power, know about the education bureaucracy, possess good communication skills, and understand about coping and grit. They can teach what Delpit (1988) referred to as "culture of power" (p. 283). Teaching students what and how to decipher academic language, to succeed in a test-taking environment, and to build the numeracy, and literacy habits and skills necessary to succeed in school, are but a few concrete examples of cultural capital.

Teachers' solid grasp of CAR as a way to generate cultural capital makes them potent agents of transformative change. Through its use they can certainly dig out the cultural capital students come with to school, augment it, and increase their exposure to more at the school.

For instance, a team of principal teacher-researchers—two social sciences and two English language—wanted to explore the teaching of complex text, as a differentiated instruction strategy, to help dual language learners—also deficit-labeled English Language Learners in the official language. The team sought to reduce the academic equity gap between these students and English only speakers. While the team framed this research project as one guided by academic concerns, the study actually was dealing with cultural capital building. Learning to decode complex text certainly falls within the notion of culture of power, in that acquiring high literacy levels offers the key to access the intricacies of dense subject matter of the science, technology, engineering, and mathematics (STEM) curriculum. When such opportunity exists, then larger numbers of students from this demographic may access advanced placement courses, thus greater chances of college going aspirations.

Following the results of a reading pre-test asking students for the main idea, and a list of supportive evidence, the assessment rubric (based on the Common Core Standards) classified test results into initial, emerging, proficient, and advanced literacy levels. As a result of the test, the team profiled a group of 62 at the initial literacy levels, and split it randomly into an experimental group of 29 and a control group of 33. The same reading pre-test was administered as post-test at the end of the action (intervention). Over a period of six weeks, the experimental group received a set of literacy strategies including: vocabulary squares, summarizing, sequencing, the five W's, before-during = after reading tactics, and

Cornell note taking templates. Complex text included titles such as: Nuremberg laws; Reconstruction; Lord of the flies; Drugs, sports, body image, and G. I. Joe.

The post-test administered after the full implementation ended six weeks later, showed these results (see Table 1.1):

Table 1.1: Pre- and Post-Reading Test

Pre-and-Post-Reading-Students' Test Results in Relative (%) Numbers

	Pre-test-Results		Post-test-Results	
Change	Experimental	Control	Experimental	Control
Positive	65	27	77	27
Negative	8	-18	0	-5
None	27	64	35	68

This small-scale study claims that the group exposed to literacy strategies improved much more than the control group: from 65% of students to 77%. That means that 12% of the students in the experimental group improved its literacy level. Eight percent of students in the same group showed a negative result in the pre-test, but none in the post-test. Still the subset of students who seems lagging in the pre-test increased by 8% in the post-test, an issue that warrants further exploration.

The researchers explain that the improvement—from -18 to a -5—"in the control group could be interpreted as natural student academic growth over time, or the difference in the reading content, which can affect students' interest and engagement." Yet, as with the lagging subset in the experimental group, the improvement of 13% of students in the control group requires further study. Learning literacy strategies to decode complex text may significantly alter the tracking out of dual language learners from college going courses.

This six-week CAR project offers a glimpse into the potential transformative power of intentionally teaching the cultural capital embedded in literacy.

Key Chapter Learning

This chapter focused on three core points: First, we outlined research as an approach that is simultaneously iterative, collaborative, adaptable, and inferential.

We also offered a three way to control bias, which is one of the main issues we encounter when studying our own institution. We then made the case for agency and agents, as sources of transformative change.

The second point delved with the collaborative component in more detail. This section shows the networking dynamics of groups and teams. We explained how forging learning communities through the intentional action of agents plays a primordial role in this research approach.

The third point presents action as a factor linked to social and cultural capital formation. Here we exposed actions invented from scratch, and actions already in place. We show how social and cultural capital are forged. They are two distinctive interlaced realities: on the one hand, social capital has to do with the value of social networks, social trust, and the creation of the common good. Cultural capital, on the other, means the representation of power, language, and social class traits—chiefly habitus. These two forms of capital may render great benefits to both, research teams and collaborators, as well as the entire organization. More importantly, in schools both forms of capital can be cultivated, and nurtured to grow among children and youth. While both forms of capital are clearly distinguishable, we also understand that cultural capital is carried out through the workings of social networks.

Throughout the chapter we emphasized the vital function of leadership as a force to promote funding, allocate resources, and stimulate team work. When this environment exists, evidence-based decision-making governs the way a human organization functions. Moreover, we posit that when intentional CAR grows into habituated and established practice, human organizations become intelligent entities, more capable of attaining their goals and objectives. It is also what makes transformative change to stay for a long term.

Essential Questions

What preconditions do we need at our working place to enact a CAR tradition? How can we use CAR to engender social and cultural capital and get rid of deficit thinking?

Activity

Social groups sit at the base of Bruce Tuckman's model. Using this model, conduct an inventory of your own or other collaboration groups functioning throughout your site. After you paint Tuckman's indicators (see below) discuss questions such as:

1. How do we explain the levels at which we have assessed our group to be in the model's continuum?
2. What do we consider as the next actions we must undertake to change the current levels?

Indicators:
Stage 1: Forming

1.1 High dependence on leader for guidance and direction.
1.2 Little agreement on team aims.
1.3 Individual roles and responsibilities are unclear.
1.4 Processes are often ignored.
1.5 Members test tolerance of system and leader.

Stage 2: Storming

2.1 Decisions don't come easily within group.
2.2 Team members vie for position as they attempt to establish themselves in relation to other team members.
2.3 Clarity of purpose increases but plenty of uncertainties persist.
2.4 Cliques and factions form and there may be power struggles.
2.5 The team still distracted by relationships and emotional issues.
2.6 Compromises may be required.
2.7 Leader coaches.
2.8 Leader continuously challenged by individual members.

Stage 3: Norming

3.1 Agreement and consensus largely forms.
3.2 Team responds well to leader's facilitation.
3.3 Roles and responsibilities are clear and accepted.

3.4 Big decisions are made by group agreement.
3.5 Smaller decisions may be delegated to individuals.
3.6 Commitment and unity is strong.
3.7 The team may engage in fun and social activities.
3.8 The team discusses and develops its processes and working style.
3.9 There is general respect for the leader and some of leadership is more shared by the team.

Stage 4: Performing

4.1 The team is more strategically aware.
4.2 The team knows clearly why it is doing what it is doing.
4.3 The team has a shared vision and is able to stand on its own feet with no interference or participation from the leader.
4.4 There is a focus on overachieving goals, and the team makes most of the decisions against criteria agreed with the leader.
4.5 The team has a high degree of autonomy.
4.6 Disagreements occur but now they are resolved within the team positively.
4.7 Changes to processes and structure are made by the team.
4.8 The team is able to work toward achieving the goal, and also to attend to relationships, style, and process issues along the way.
4.9 Team members look after each other.
4.10 The team requires delegated tasks and projects from the leader.
4.11 The team does not need to be instructed or assisted.
4.12 Team members might ask for assistance from the leader with personal and interpersonal development.
4.13 Leader delegates and oversees.

From: Tuckman B. (1975) Team developmental model Downloaded 12/09/2019 from https://www.businessballs.com/team-management/tuckman-forming-storming-norming-performing-model/

Resources

The Professional Learning Association
https://learningforward.org/standards/learning-communities/

Center for Collaborative Action Research
http://cadres.pepperdine.edu/ccar/define.html
Association for Interdisciplinary Studies
https://i2s.anu.edu.au/resources/association-interdisciplinary-studies
Action Research Network for the Americas
https://i2s.anu.edu.au/resources/action-research-network-americas

References

Apple, M. W. (2004). *Ideology and curriculum*. New York, NY: Routledge.
Arriaza, G., & Rocha, C. (2014). Growing social capital in the classroom. *Issues in Teacher Education Journal, 25*(1), 59–71.
Bourdieu, P. (1986). The forms of capital. In J. C. Richardson (Ed.), *Handbook of theory and research for the sociology of education* (pp. 241–258). New York, NY: Greenwood Press.
Delpit, L. (1988). The silenced dialogue: Power and pedagogy in educating other people's children. *Harvard Educational Review, 58*(3), 280–299.
Dumais, S. (2005). Early childhood cultural capital, parental habitus, and teachers' perceptions. *Poetics, 43*, 83–107.
Freire, P. (1966). *La educación como práctica de la libertad*. Siglo XXI. Mexico DF, Mexico.
Gould, S. J. (1996). *The measure of man*. New York, NY: W. W. Norton, Co.
Jonassen, D. H., & Rohrer-Murphy, L. (1999). Activity theory as a framework for designing constructivist learning environments. *Educational Technology Research and Development, 47*(1), 61–79.
Kandel, E. R. (2007). *In search of memory. The emergence of a new science of mind*. New York, NY: W.W. Norton and Co.
Lewin, K. (1946). Action research and minority problems. *Journal of Social Issues, 2*(4), 34–46.
Maturana, H. R., & Varela, F. J. (1987). *The tree of knowledge. The biological roots of human understanding*. Boston, MA: Shambhala Publications, Co.
Tramonte, L., & Willms, J. D. (2010). Cultural capital and its effects on education outcomes. *Economics of Education Review, 29*(2), 200–213.
Tuckman, B. W. (1965). Developmental sequence in small groups. *Psychological Bulletin, 63*(6), 384–399.

2

The Challenge

The cycle of inquiry is a vehicle to a more democratic institution, one that makes site-based decisions on the voices of the many rather than the few. Socially responsible leaders utilize the cycle of inquiry to promote school improvement by empowering teachers to identify a challenge, using the inquiry process to see all of the moving parts that are barriers to change [. . .] The root of our inquiry question originated from our day-to-day experiences in the classroom. Using Collaborative Action Research (CAR), we found that we all had a voice throughout the inquiry process, because there were built-in reflection phases during the cycle. In the end, the research was fully developed because of the many layers. Ultimately, because of the integrity and collaboration of the study, we felt a shared ownership of the solutions.

What does this mean for us as leaders? We have identified that teachers learn by doing— cycling through the collaborative action research – and by giving teachers the time to cycle through this process. It illuminates the many facets of the school and raises awareness of the subtle nuances that go into just one aspect of the school community. Through CAR, teachers are more apt to support school programs that have been vetted through this cycle.

Another area of growth stemmed from connections between our inquiry and what it means to be a socially responsible leader. A bold leader has the ability to holistically identify and serve the needs of the larger school community. Through our specific study, we witnessed the impact that fostering the relationship between parent, teacher, and student had in the classroom. As a leader, building relationships and fostering innovation is what invigorates social change in the school community.

Katelyn LaPine, Kelly Noriega, and Jennifer Rohrbach (personal communication)

CAR, Culture, Climate, and Structure

CAR engenders local production of knowledge, its collective sharing, and the ownership of the responses and solutions to the challenges it uncovers. The research team of LaPine, Noriega, and Rohrbach, cited above, define this social ecosystem as "one that makes site-based decisions on the voices of the many rather than the few." This methodology certainly produces a cascading effect in an organization, such as, as this research team points out, the democratization of knowledge.

The researcher-practitioners additionally state that CAR methodology empowers teachers "to identify a challenge, using the inquiry process to see all of the moving parts that are barriers to change." Defining the challenge, as they stated, plays a major function in collaborative action research. It is the point of departure, the first step of the methodology, and a constant presence throughout. A research effort, indeed, hinges upon the accuracy of the identified challenge, which relies entirely on the available evidence.

A challenge manifests through a series of effects documented as lived experience, perceptions, or indicators measuring the empirical reality. Thus, any attempt identifying a challenge includes a diverse set of evidentiary material, as well as the availability of technologies to implement an appropriate research process, a supportive and well-coordinated organizational culture, and leadership capacity at all levels.

Defining the nature of a challenge includes a clear understanding of the social, organizational, and cultural environment within which said challenge exists. This is so because identifying the right challenge the right way, may determine the future of an organization's performance. This is inquiry's zero point of departure, and its function is analogous to a compass in navigation. Setting and controlling the guidance systems correctly will direct a ship to the port of destination with great accuracy. A slight mistake would very likely send it to the wrong place. In Columbus days, the discovery of a clock to exactly calculate longitude was not yet available. Fifteenth century naval explorers, like Columbus, often got lost in the vast oceans. He thought he had arrived in India. Thus, as a compass guides a ship, the definition of the challenge leads inquiry in a human organization.

An inquiry project follows these two coordinates—the challenge and the question. The challenge builds a case by describing an issue of great importance to the organization; such description conveys a compelling argument substantiated by the available evidence. The question(s) synthesizes the challenge and ties it to a potential inquiry methodology.

As suggested above, to successfully plan and conduct a research project, four core elements ought to be present: a supportive and functional organizational practice; leadership capacity at all levels; a robust, diverse, and available set of evidentiary materials; and the availability of technologies to implement an appropriate collaborative action research. Functional organizational practice, and leadership capacity pertain to culture; data sets, and technology belong to structures.

Before we continue, let's make a quick pause here to remind us the meanings of, first, culture, and then, structure. Bowel (1966) coined organizational culture as the way things are done. In the realm of business, Bowel looked at culture as the ultimate explanation of corporate success, and in a way, his concern was focused on patterned habits, and the pragmatism of running a big organization. While considering behavior a vital part of organizational culture, our understanding of culture is broader—it includes the traditions, symbols, beliefs, and values that, like the foundation of a building, cement social relations. Habermas (1988) tied culture to language—the communicative means—and defined this whole environment as life world.

Culture, though, is different to climate in that, the latter consists of the subjective relation between individuals and the whole of the organization. It conveys more of a feeling about the place, and it is the first thing that greets visitors. Freiberg and Stein (1999) described it as the soul and heart of a school. It is what makes the place attractive, engaging, one where we want to be in and work, or not.

Structure, on the other hand, refers to the systems, procedures, and government of an organization. As Daft (2004), and Huang, Rode & Schroeder (2011) have shown, organizational structures distribute power and responsibilities, and play a central role in the organizations' capacity to improve and learn. These attributes make up the key conduits for an organization's culture to exist. Without structure an organization cannot exert its functions. Akin to a building's columns, floors, and walls that rise up firmly tethered to a foundation, structures and culture are tightly linked, and one cannot think of them as autonomous parts of an organization, Habermas (1988) called the whole of structures, system world.

The Focal Issue

First of all, we use the term "challenge," instead of problem, to convey the idea that when researching we embark ourselves in a journey of discovery. Challenge implies struggle, search for root level causes of the issue affecting our work. The term "problem" may suggest that somehow, we already know the forces, or factors determining a phenomenon and, therefore, presupposes the availability of a solution, a treatment.

We aim at rallying support through understanding.

The definition of the challenge consists of a convincing argument about its potential significance. We want people to understand the challenge's likely crucial value added to the entire organization. Thus, the challenge's merits sit front and center in our defining efforts. This process, then, does not leave room for doubt, confusion, or even reasons for the readers to hesitate and thus deny their support. Therefore, the language we use ought to be as direct, precise, persuasive, and unambiguously articulated. We have come to think of it as a process similar to building a case in a court of law.

A persuasive definition of the challenge must contain uncontroversial evidence that substantiates every single claim we make. In order to move an audience to embrace the case, we cite the relevant evidence to prove the challenge exists in all its details and ramifications.

For instance, the claim:

> Too many children from low socio-economic background do not continue higher education after graduating from high school.

It should be immediately followed with an actual data statement, such as:

> According to a report from the national center of education statistics – NCES - (2018). over the last ten years, about only fourteen percent of graduates from this social background continue on to a four-year college education.

An opening statement such as this example and, in general, the entire definition of the challenge must strike a balance between advocacy and scholarly detachment. While we may be quite personally involved, the need to restrain our natural tendency to advocate becomes even more serious. We want and must avoid readers' dismissal based on perceived bias. Here is where the more detached and, to the extent possible, neutral position of a traditional researcher comes handy. Being cognizant of the tension of this dual identity is particularly decisive for education leaders, and this is so because planning to study their own practices is like critically seeing oneself on the mirror—it collapses professional role with emotional involvement. And the picture we see might not be attractive.

Back to our example, the words "too," and "only" may prove problematic. The final editing could substitute them with less compromising terms. Since they may convey bias, crossing them out of the statement may help us to gain a more balanced assertion even if it is true that, in our personal opinion, *too* many students don't continue higher education, and that *only* a few make it.

"*Many* children from low socio-economic background do not continue higher education after graduating from high school. According to a report from the National Center of Education Statistics—NCES—(2018), over the last ten years about fourteen percent of graduates from this social strata continue on to a four-year college education."

The statement, nevertheless, misses a fundamental component: *scope*.

As currently written, one can interpret it as a countrywide issue, since the definition lacks precise boundaries. Defining the problem implies a clear size. As zooming to take a picture of a hill in springtime, we may have three frames: first the entire hill, second a section of the hill with the most flowers, and third a patch of bright yellowish and orange California poppies. An effective definition of the challenge may then start at the state level, like Texas; then narrow it down to a region, such as Austin's metropolitan area, then a concrete school district like Lake Travis Independent School District, and finally a specific school, for instance Serene Hills Elementary, or a small set of schools selected by, say, a shared concern around the access of girls to algebra.

Back to our example, if we start at the national level, honing the definition on a concrete school means that we need to go down to the state, then the district, and finally, the school levels. The same statement above, but with a clear national-level scope would read like this:

> Many children from low socio-economic background in the United States do not continue higher education after graduating from high school. According to a report from the National Center of Education Statistics – NCES - (2018), over the last ten years, about fourteen percent of graduates from this social strata in the country continue on to a four-year college education.

What comes next is the comparable statistics at the state level, and further reduce the scope from there to the specific school district, and then the school(s).

Besides a well-balanced and persuasive tone, we keep the audience at the center of our intentions. In other words, we make a case specifically directed to a clearly identified group of readers, and not to the world. Keeping in mind these individuals and their roles in the institution forces us to reason in the most effective way possible.

Typically, defining the challenge targets decision makers and faculty. Decision makers, such as school administrators, district office, local, county, and state boards, allocate budgets, distribute resources, and enact policy. We need them to seriously first consider our concerns and second join us by supporting our efforts. The other targeted audience is our colleagues since they are the end users of the results of the action research, and the long-term partners most impacted before, during, and after the action research. Staff involvement also determines the study's scale.

We distinguish two scale areas here: one refers to the participants' mind frame, and the other to sheer number of participants. Collaborative action research conceives any study as one that places the entire organization as the ultimate goal. That is to say that regardless of the type of challenge being undertaken, the orientation of both the purpose and the use of the results looks at the whole institution. In this sense, an action research involving, for instance, one classroom is considered a microscopic sample of the entire organization. The results of a study focused on literacy in only that classroom aims at illuminating literacy challenges in the entire institution.

The number of participants is also called unit of analysis. A team of two researchers,—the smallest collaboration unit—and their two classrooms of, say, thirty students each, determines the scale of the unit of analysis. The unit of analysis here is a small one—two classrooms. Check Chapter One where we covered the teams' disciplinary variations and also examined possible combinations.

A pair of teachers studying literacy challenges in their classrooms may mean that the results of the inquiry will chiefly impact their classrooms, but when the results of the study are shared, that of others whose concerns and challenges the inquiry mirrors, will also benefit. When the scale of the unit of analysis is larger, such as a collaborative action research involving a whole set of classrooms, or the entire institution, may have a different, perhaps greater, impact.

Identification: Learning and Cultural Habits

When defining the challenge, we ask ourselves whether such challenge is a manifestation of something deeper, or the actual root-level factors. Argyris (1982, 2002) proposes that identifying the governing variables of an issue leads to greater chances of success. This author presents a challenge identification model that forces us to go beyond the examination of our actions and their resulting effects.

Modifying our actions to change results is called single loop. But Argyris proposes a double loop learning as the most effective intentional learning method, one that requires us to examine the root level factors governing the challenge. We first observe the results of the action we have been involved in, as first loop, but then we must look at what is beneath it—the variables governing the situation. Argyris uses the following example: when a thermostat, set at certain degrees, "turns the heat on or off, it is acting in keeping with the program of orders given to it to keep the room temperature," (1982, p. 4) at the degrees it was set. If the technology malfunctions, we may simply replace the thermostat with a new one. This is single loop. But if instead, we dig deeper into the machine's programs that made the thermostat to malfunction, we are then addressing learning as a double loop.

See Figure 2.1 as an illustration:

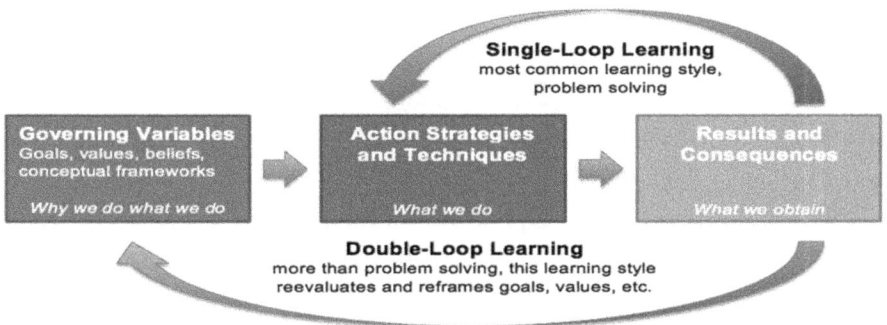

Figure 2.1: Double loop learning
Source: http://www.invistaperforms.org/wp-content/uploads/2017/01/loop-learning1.png
Downloaded Jan. 12, 2020.

Similar to Argyris' proposal, Henze, Katz, & Norte (2001) advance an "iceberg" model as a learning strategy for the identification of a challenge. They note that "[m]ost of us have been conditioned to work from the assumption that overt challenges are the ones that need fixing" (p. 45). Instead, they propose to look beyond what is obvious and to distinguish three layers:

1. Above the surface, where overt conflict resides (such as day-to-day emotional and physical aggression).
2. Below the surface, which consists of a middle level loaded with latent conflicts that may or may not find a way to express themselves (such as accumulated resentment, or prevailing stereotypes).
3. A deeper layer at the root level of conflict (such as economic segregation, power imbalance, and cultural marginalization).

Henze et al. advocate for the need to search at the third layer if one wants to engage in learning at the causal level, and to make enduring organizational change. Embracing Argyris' or Henze's et al. approaches may produce great benefits to an organization's learning efforts. The process may certainly yield a more nuanced understanding of reality.

We have invested our energies and emotions for a period of time at work, and now it is time to study the results. It is only natural that participants reject or at least resist the data in front of them when no traditions and habits of evidence examination exist. An organization's culture, though, is forged through practice. We create habits by acting. Start with the facilitation of evidence analysis sessions.

Facilitating this examination of the evidence requires skill. The facilitator needs to select an appropriate process. Here is a brief list of some of the most popular ones: the logic model, gap analysis, fishbone analysis, the five whys, Socratic method. They all follow a systematic step-by-step, intentional, participatory, and logical process. Selecting a particular process should be made according to the organization's cultural profile.

We next list a set of guiding principles for the examination of evidence at all times. When we initiate the identification of a challenge, we ultimately seek to uncover its governing variables. From this floor-level premise, we follow these six core-guiding principles:

1. Defining a challenge means that we are not trying to find solutions.
   When examining the evidence, avoid formulating conclusions, and proposing solutions. Let the evidence speak by itself. This is so simple because we actually do not know the true nature of root-level factors that have produced the challenge. The work in schools, universities, health centers, social work, and other social-service oriented professions come with a

heavy doses of advocacy. In schools, educators spend a significant amount of time in a problem-solving mode. This is called "the tyranny of the urgent."

Overpowered by what is urgent, solving what is important takes backstage. In this sense, the act of studying the evidence in our quest for understanding a challenge, may prove difficult, to say the least. It takes patience and time.

Being cognizant of our advocacy tendencies come here handy the rule of thumb: state only what the evidence shows.

2. *Defining a challenge means that we pursue the understanding of the factors at the base of the challenge.*

    Our analysis of the evidence seeks to comprehend the challenge. Pinpointing the closest factors at the root level of a challenge is not an easy task. In the social realm, we encounter multiple and confounding forces, acting simultaneously, at times overlapping.

    Indeed, what may constitute cause for a concrete issue may actually be the effect of another, and likewise, what may be the effect of an issue can actually be the cause of another. Moreover, multiple causes may produce one effect, as well as multiple effects may be the result of one cause.

    Add a timeline to this complexity.

    How far back in time do we want to go? These considerations must be determined based on an institution's needs. They also make the challenge a challenge. We visit this issue later in this chapter, under section "evidence." *The rule of thumb: hone in on the one factor you bet will produce the biggest impact, and fix data collection to a reasonable point (year, or event) on the calendar.*

3. *Defining the challenge means checking our work against the institution's mission and vision.*

    We want to see what differences exist between what we have stated we believe in value espoused, and what we actually have done. In other words, study the evidence in terms of our espoused values and beliefs, against what we actually practice. Finding gaps in this comparative activity should not surprise anyone. Rather, the gap's size and its makeup should surprise us (see Figure 2.2).

44 | *Community-Owned Knowledge*

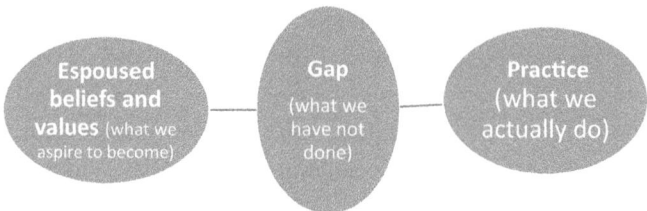

Figure 2.2: Gap analysis
Source G. Arriaza © 2020

The scope of this analysis may be bounded by two work areas: First, we may want to take only one part of the espoused beliefs and values (usually expressed in a vision statement and a mission statement). Second, we must bound the analysis by the challenge we want to address.

The first step of this gap analysis process consists of taking the espoused beliefs and values statements sentence by sentence. The second step consists of isolating the operative concepts further, as a way to simplify the process. The third step of the process consists of probing questions about the issue we want to investigate.

Example

Let's take only the vision statement:

We commit to serving students up to their full potential, and do whatever it takes to eliminate academic gaps, including college readiness.

First step: Two sentences: 1) We commit to serving all students to their full potential; 2) [We commit to] do whatever it takes to eliminate academic gaps, including college readiness.

Second step: Operative concepts: 1) serving all, 2) full potential, 3) eliminate gaps, 4) college readiness.

Third step: Isolate the component linked to our research interest. In this example we could ask: How are we doing with "college readiness"?

What follows next is the close analysis of the available evidence regarding college going. At the end of this process, we should have a set of indicators telling us how we are doing.

The rule of thumb: bound a gap analysis by linking the espoused beliefs and values (vision and mission statements) to the challenge the action research has zeroed-in.

4. *Defining the challenge means a close look at our work with no blaming and guilt tripping.*
As an illustration, let's repeat here an old story from an unknown author:
The college professor said,
"Such rawness in a student is a shame.
Lack of preparation in the high school is to blame."
Said the high school teacher,
"Good Heavens! That boy's a fool.
The fault, of course, is with the middle school."
The middle school teacher said,
"From such stupidity, may I be spared.
They sent him up so unprepared."
The primary teacher huffed,
"Kindergarten blockheads all.
They call that preparation—why it's worse than none at all."
The kindergarten teacher said,
"Such lack of training, never did I see.
What kind of woman must that mother be?"
The mother said,
"Poor helpless child. He's not to blame.
His father's people were all the same."
Said the father, at the end of the line,
"I doubt the rascal's even mine."

Looking at the evidence raises expectations and anxieties at the same time. Seeing these data show the results of our dedicated work, the product of our daily efforts. The entangled emotions of our labor's sweat and facts (such as an end-of-year test, a testimony, or a report on suspensions) may trigger deep feelings of guilt. But then also, they may lead us to externalize responsibility—who to blame. Guilt makes us feel uneasy at best, blinding us from a frank review of the evidence in front of us. Who is blamed usually will very likely reject the accusation.

Good facilitation focuses on the evidence as presented, and steers the conversation away from these two powerful feelings. Otherwise, the debilitating effects of guilt and blame may certainly induce paralysis to the process, and in the end stifle participants' professional growth. Even if we may feel less efficacious at what we do, we seek to move forward by learning from our shortcomings. Flipping guilt into acceptance of our responsibility opens the opportunity to grow.

The rule of thumb: eradicate feelings of guilt and blame, and embrace responsibility.

5. *Defining the challenge means bringing in all the types of evidence available at the moment.*

    As in nature, diversity strengthens a human organization. Counting with diverse data points allows us to look at the issues from as many angles as possible. Thus, while we proceed with the evidence we got, we need to gather as much as possible. Nonetheless, the need for exploring more evidentiary material tends to prevail in data analysis sessions. This fact cannot be ignored. Any new evidence should come in when available and if appropriate. Yet, the work must continue forward. When petitions for more evidence arise, it helps having a careful record of each piece requested, and when it was requested, who volunteered to look for it, and the potential sources to obtain it. Sometimes these notes are written on a place easy for all participants to see. Some call these parking lot notes.

    In other words, an explicit commitment to move forward with the evidence available forms part of the organization's culture, and it must be practiced at all times. Not operating in this manner inevitably pushes the work off the rails. A popular saying fits here: endless analysis leads to paralysis.

    The rule of thumb: move forward with the evidence available at the moment.

6. *Defining the challenge means focusing on internal issues as a lever to enact change.*

    Without ignoring external issues, locating the challenge within the institution itself provides a potent leverage to enact transformative change. Any effort to identify a challenge must first prioritize the issues within the organization, the internal ones, and place those outside as complement. Next, the identification process must hone in on the internal issues to which we have full access, and at the same time we hold a high degree of control. These are the focal issues. We detail this issue some more in the section "evidence" below.

    Key in the selection and embrace of the focal issues is the expert assessment of those closest to them. The calculation involved in this choice is one similar to betting. We cannot claim with absolute certainty that what we have chosen as the challenge will produce the best results. We expect to have identified the most promising leverage, the one that will help move the entire organization. As Archimedes' law of the lever tells us—give me a long enough lever and a place to stand, and I'll move the world. We revisit this point in the section below on evidence.

The rule of thumb: chose an internal issue with the most promise for transformative change.

Example:
Let's summarize this section's points with the following case.

A few years ago, a team of five school leaders from a comprehensive high school in San José, California, launched a collaborative action research. They first discovered that graduating classes over the last three years met the requirements—also known as the A through G list—necessary for admission in either the California State, or the University of California systems. Yet, compared to the year prior to enforcing A through G requirements to all students, the number of college applicants had remained static. The school staff had been successful at implementing the school district mission: ensure all students meet the A–G list by 12th grade. But from ninth-to-twelfth grade classrooms, there was no talk, activities, information available about the value of a college education, nor organized efforts, except for the counseling office, to show students how to apply to college. After examining all data available, the team decided that a possible root cause of the challenge had to do with the absence of a college going culture. Second, the team shared these insights with school administrators who wholeheartedly supported the efforts.

Next, the team concluded that to forge a culture, they needed to intentionally teach about college. They created a vocabulary, and a set of key habits for ninth graders. The team determined to spiral-build from their more complex topics in the 10th and 11th to aiding 12th graders to learn about economics of higher education, and how to apply to college. The advisory, or zero period, became the venue to develop and implement the college-going curriculum. The plan aimed at having the first substantial results in three years, when current ninth graders would be juniors, and ready to start planning to go on to college.

The teacher leaders sought longitudinal evidence (three years), and focused on the number of college applicants, academic records, teachers' testimonies, and students' own stories about college. After weighing a series of factors, such as family's college education, students' social behavior, friendship groups, and teachers' beliefs about college education, they laser-focused on the lack of college going talk among the entire faculty. From this point on, the teachers enlisted the school administrators' support who, in turn, made the zero-period advisory the slated time for the team's action.

Once the team created a curriculum that, they hypothesized, would start building from ninth grade on, a tradition and talk of college going, the action was launched. Two points played a crucial role in this case: First, the team counted with the school administration's support; second, team members trusted their capacity to earn the majority of the school staff's support.

Other than a few adjustments, the action was successfully implemented, so much so that the district's central administration recruited the team to bring their curriculum to the other high schools.

As we can see here, the team stayed focused on an internal issue. They were betting and concentrated their efforts on a very specific component: lack of college going talk, traditions. While parental education appeared as very important, the team considered this fact as an external, complementary issue.

Furthermore, the team enjoyed full access and the trust of the school staff. This fact allowed teachers to keep the locus of control.

Locating the time period to start and follow the evidence in this example has to do more with the specific circumstances of a particular study than with a general rule. We have learned that the timeline depends on the profile of the challenge being studied. The team in our story located the year to the one prior to when the school started to purposefully and systematically teach and track the course work of the A through G list. Other studies may not necessarily have to collect longitudinal data.

Bottom line here—timeframes are determined by the contours of a challenge, the study's specific needs and purposes, and availability of resources to conduct the study.

Finally, the team could have chosen anything out of a full array of challenges, since these abound in high schools. They selected one that, in the abstract, may not seem as important as, say, mathematics, or English language performance—the two gatekeepers of higher education. The team reasoned that after a few years of emphasizing the A–G requirements, the school still was not producing the desired results—proportionally low college applications. The staff could keep pushing more mathematics and English instruction, but still the number of college applications would not have budged. So the question became—what challenge is there that, if we understand and act upon, will render the greatest benefit to students and the institution as a whole?

Selecting a cultural issue had to do with a series of assumptions and calculations, all of which belong to the realm of subjective assessment of the objective reality, and less to do with a linear, cold, and predictable analysis. Thus, besides asking about how internal, and how much access and control one may have on an issue, a vital concern is maximizing the use of time, as well as staff talent and skill.

Sharpening the action research on college going culture meant betting at this factor (call it governing variable) as the best possible answer to the question of the lever above. Most action research pivots on a decision of this nature. We haven't found a formula that would lead us to perfection. We rather trust the process, the available evidence, and our collective capacity to decipher the meanings buried in the evidence.

Situating the Issue

After the principal research team has honed in on a challenge, what comes next is understanding where it is located, and what it actually is made out of. As with everything in social life, the challenge originates, lives, and grows somewhere in the culture and the social milieu. Everything happens within such realm. The challenge breaths in and out in a given context. Thus, understanding the contours and detailed make-up of the challenge will help us to fully comprehend it. Consequently, accurately situating the challenge is of great significance for a successful action research.

Situating a problem includes at least five different spheres.

Academic Context: It may include everything dealing with the content, delivery, pace, sequence, and assessment of curriculum. This sphere sits at the top of schools' priorities, and deals with what adults, and students learn, and how they do learn. Having clear and precise data of the academic life may allow us access to performance indicators revealing pedagogical practices, cognitive issues, and belief and value systems. Disaggregating these data—such as graduation rates, disciplinary actions, GPA, college going rates, and demography—and by key categories—such as gender, socioeconomic, ethnicity, and native language—unlocks a wide-open window into the core mission of the institution.

As we stated earlier, we must pay attention to the scope of these data. As in photography, we direct our narrowest lens by zooming in on the specific groups or individual students who show the sharpest manifestation of the challenge we want to research. After we have analyzed these data, we need to then open the lens a little more, from this ground level to the whole institution. From here we can build our understanding of the problem within the context of the entire organization. Next, we need to widen the lens some more to comparable institutions.

Depending on the purposes of the research project, we may compare the institution to other local ones, whether within the same school district or others. Again, from this level now, we widen the aperture even more to include the county, state, and country. Keep in mind: we compare data reflecting the same issue. If the concern, for instance, is graduation rates of a specific demographic, we will look at this issue at the school, local, state, and national levels.

Social Context: Describing the social context comprises the social life within the institution as well as its surrounding communities. It refers to the nature of relationships, and to the type and functions of social networks (e.g., friendship groups, clicks, and virtual networks).

Social context also describes power hierarchies (e.g., economic stability, housing, businesses, and elected local offices), and other key features such as social cohesion (e.g., common good, social trust, and wealth), social distance, and income distribution as reflection of social class. It also comprises social behavior recorded by the school as disciplinary incidents, conflict engagement, restorative resolutions to conflict and health—physical and emotional—support.

The U.S. Census, municipal records, the school district, and the state department of education may help with these data points.

Cultural Context: It contains languages (linguistic diversity, and country of origin), traditions (fairs, celebrations, values, and symbols), habituated behaviors, and rites. Cultural context also includes the cultivation of traits that carry some currency in society and how these are negotiated by all members of the organization. In schools, cultural context involves the identification of those activities that adults engage purposefully to introduce students to museums, art, music, other artistic expressions, and educational institutions otherwise unavailable to them.

It also refers to intellectual (e.g., reading, writing, and numeracy) pursuits, and physical habits (i.e., sports) that trace the fulfillment of the whole person as a critical and healthy thinking entity. Describing culture implicates the social context, since these mutually feed each other. We separated the social and cultural context here for explanatory reasons. In reality, this section of the research project should be labeled social and cultural context.

Organization and Systems Context: Also called structures, organization, and systems refer to the actual functioning, and inner workings of the organization. It describes the lines of operation for members of the organization, the steps followed to make, execute, and evaluate decisions. It also includes the logistics necessary for the organization to be functional—how acquisitions work, how services are delivered, the interface of the different components, such as in the case of parental involvement in fundraising, how the school teaching cadre muster community resources and use these directly to the last consumer—students; and how the school administration develops coherence between concrete student needs and the multiple affiliations with stake holders, technical assistance providers, state, and local government agencies.

A central structural component of the context has to do with existing data systems, their interface with district and state databases, and their actual use by teachers and administrators.

Environmental Context: The challenge schools face addressing their CO_2 footprint has increased and accelerated over the last decade. The environmental context involves addressing the use of energy, type of building and classroom materials, location of the schools' physical buildings, learning about and the civic duty of acting to deal with the cascading effects of environmental degradation, the critical engagement of consumption, food production, distribution, and eating habits.

Environmental context has to do with the well-being of all members of the organization, the degrees of fulfillment, and happiness as expressed by the quality of the food and water available, the type of sustainability of the buildings, and the existing accommodations. It also considers the ways the collaborative action research challenge relates to the three R's: reduce, reuse, and recycle.

Example

Note that describing context depends on the nature of the challenge the principal research team has determined on to zero in the research project. Thus, the spheres and their components must always be relevant to the challenge. Context data that do not add any value to locating the challenge have no place in the description of the context. Let's emphasize here a core truism in research:

The context must describe the academic (in the case of learning institutions), social, cultural, organizational, and environmental spheres where the problem exists.

For clarity purposes, we have included with this example two parts: first, the definition of the challenge (or the focal issue) and second, the description of the context.

1. Definition of the Challenge:
   Amy Marymor, Mirel Rivera, and Kira Walsh—a collaborative research team working on reading gaps in the upper grades of elementary education—after a granular-level analysis of the academic data, concluded:

[I]t is evident that the biggest area of concern is reading. The largest disparity seems to be in the transition between third and fourth grade, where student scores drop significantly from the previous year.

And they went on arguing:

The current fourth graders are already behind in their reading skills. A district-wide reading assessment supports the SBAC findings in reading (see Table 3). The discrepancy in the average reading level of each class is well below grade level, ranging from a year and one month to two years one month below.

Then the authors continue making their point this way:

In the upper grades literacy becomes essential as children transition from learning to read to reading to learn. As Slavin (2011) stated, upper elementary students must "consolidate and extend their basic skills, to be sure, and they must become fluent, confident readers." (p. 9) The Smarter Balanced Assessment System (SBAC) - which tests the Common Core standards - uses a high degree of language in the mathematics assessment. Students must be able to read and comprehend test questions and write out explanations of their conceptual thinking.

The researchers seal their discussion with an irrefutable assertion:

This lag in reading levels will continue and likely widen through school and will ultimately be a disadvantage in life unless this issue is addressed. As Hernandez (2011) stated, "struggling readers rarely catch up with their peers academically and are four times more likely to drop out of high school, lowering their earning power as adults and possibly costing society in welfare and other supports." (p. 1)

2. Situating the Issue:
   As the text above shows, the Marymor, Rivera & Walsh team always substantiated their claims with data and literature references. Not one point escaped their careful argumentation. The researchers clearly defined the challenge within the academic sphere, and then they nestled it within the school's and the city's demographics
   Here is how they succinctly described the context:

Coronado Elementary is located in a large city, in a low-income, densely populated neighborhood demarcated by three different train tracks, which give to it its nickname - iron triangle. The campus was recently rebuilt and opened in fall of 2015, as a community service school. It features a dental facility along with an art, music, multi-purpose, and science rooms, as well as a computer lab, and a room equipped with a stage that can double as dance classroom. School-wide enrichment activities such as an after-school program, music, Playworks, Toolbox, and Mindful Life are also available. The site has drawn so many new families to enroll that classrooms are at maximum enrollment.

The student population is comprised of 64% Hispanic students, 27% African American, 3% Asian, 2% Pacific Islander, 2% White and less than 1% Filipino. The site is a full Title 1 - 95% of the students qualify for free or reduced lunch (GreatSchools, 2016); English Language Learners make up 49%, and students identified with disabilities make up 9% (SEIS, 2016). Overall, 25% of all students are proficient in English/ Language Arts, while 18% are proficient in Math (CDE, 2016).

According to the district's contract, maximum class size for kindergarten through third grade classes is 28 students; fourth through sixth grade classes, including combination classes, are capped at 33. Currently, the school has combination classes in two secondary classrooms: there are two full fourth grade classes, a four/five combination class, a full fifth, a five/ six combination, and a full sixth grade. All upper grade classes hold 32–33 students.

Such class-size numbers exceed what, among others, the National Council of Teachers of English (2016) has found: students in smaller classes perform better than in bigger classes, especially in elementary school.

As the graph below illustrates the current low performance in literacy of third through sixth graders in language arts (ELA) of the Smarter Balanced Assessment System (SBAC). In third grade, more than three- fourths (82%) of the students scored at level one. In fourth grade, more than two thirds (67%) of the students scored at level one as well. The sixth grade class, the highest performing grade, less than half the students have met or exceeded ELA proficiency.

54 | *Community-Owned Knowledge*

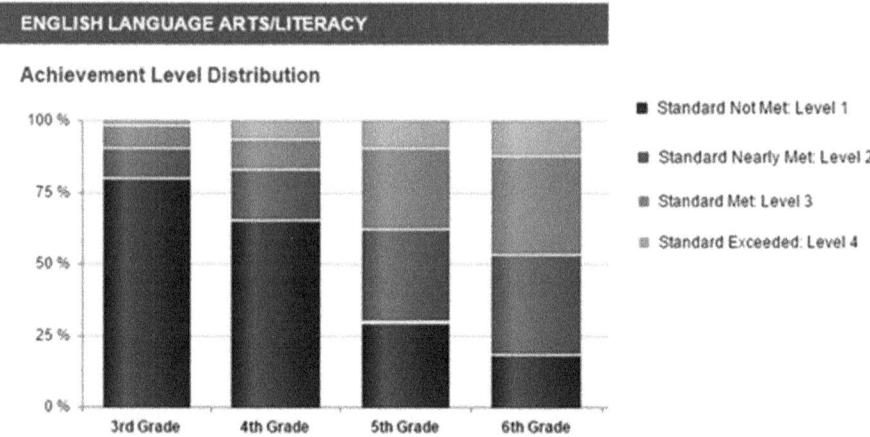

Figure 2.3: Smarter balanced results
Source: SBAC. ELA results. Created by Marymor, Rivera & Walsh, 2018.

The team closes the case with an unambiguous statement, emphasizing the already defined problem:

> After we have further investigated these test scores, it is evident that the biggest area of concern is reading.

The Action

Describing the context in which the challenge exists includes the actions designed to address the challenge. But we discuss this point as a separate section from context, given its relevance.

The action offers an opportunity for learning. Indeed, a full understanding of the challenge depends on how clearly we can formulate a theory of action, how we can outline the goals and objectives of the action, and how we can align the material and human resources invested, timelines, indicators, and the target population, to the goals.

As we explained in Chapter One, an action may be one the institution already implemented and that may need some interrogation, or it can be one the principal research team and the rest of the supporting research teams may need to create and implement from the ground up.

The components outlined next apply to an action weather it already exists or that ought to be created. Principal research teams need to look into the institution's plans, and dig into all evidentiary sources necessary to be able to pinpoint exactly the type, nature, and implications of any action, which are typically called "interventions." We will use both terms interchangeably.

Once clearly understood, an action plan may contain (see an organizer sample at the end of chapter):

1. Goals and Objectives
   These are, respectively, long- and short-term accomplishments. Goals mean the generic outcomes defined as attainable over a long period of time. Objectives mean the concrete, short term, and measurable outcomes. We measure the success or failure of each goal by achieving the stated objectives. In other words, we attain our goals through explicit and doable objectives.
   The research project's own schedule will consider the intervention's goals and objectives timetable, and calibrate its own process to include the data generated by the intervention. This implies that, at pre-established intervals (for instance, the date agreed upon to check the status of an objective, or the date when an objective is due), data are analyzed and presented to the institution's staff. At these data sessions, the principal research team will very likely hear feedback about the data, the process, and the results. Sometimes the feedback may confirm the work, and the only move consists of pushing forward. But, the team may hear constructive feedback that might request to redesign the procedures, search for new evidence, and even rework the definition of the problem and the research question(s). As we stated in Chapter One, the adaptable nature of collaborative action research lends its flexibility and capacity to take feedback in, adjust, and keep moving.
2. Background and Baseline Data
   The principal research team gathers the intervention's background data: values and principles, how the intervention approaches match the defined challenge, performance history and evidence, and sponsorship. Equal consideration must go to clearly profiling the target population the intervention purports to benefit
   Baseline data hold a crucial value. These allow the team to know the status of the participants *BEFORE* the implementation of the intervention. These

data make it possible to compare participants' progress *THROUGH* the time the intervention lasts, and the results *AFTER* the intervention ends.
3. Material and Human Resources
Mapping out the material resources invested, the money and time going into the intervention's effort, as well as the individuals and their functions and responsibilities, play an outmost importance for any research project.
4. Theory of Action
Whether explicitly stated, the principal research team needs to have understanding of the underlying assumption of the intervention's rationale. We propose that formulating a theory of action may be quite useful, so that to synthesize said assumption.

Resulting from the analysis of the evidence a theory of action is a basic three-part proposition:

If ... Then ... So that ...,

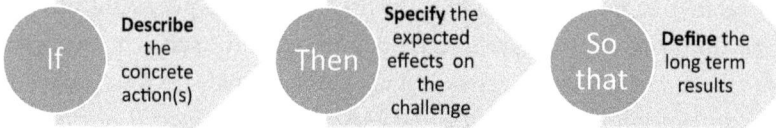

Figure 2.4: Theory of action
Source G. Arriaza © 2020

Example:
The Marymor, Rivera & Walsh principal researchers team realized no action had been taken by the school. They then created their own, original literacy intervention.
Here is how they went about this:

> We determined that to address the literacy gap – as we discussed it in the definition of the challenge – objective-setting could be a powerful intervention. Learning-goal-setting, we theorized, would most definitely move our students to close the distance between where their reading skills were, to where these should be at.

1. Goals and Objectives:
   We decided that the goal of our intervention was to close the literacy equity gap. Our objective consisted of the following: teach children how to set concrete reading levels, as a doable objective.
   Beginning in December of this year, one of us led a focus group—a 4th/5th grade combination class—through a goal setting process in which students would set specific personal reading objectives. We asked them to first look at their reading levels, and second we taught them how to review and understand their respective reading levels.
   Later, we instructed them on how to write a realistic reading objectives. We checked that each of these was attainable and that each would fit the proper format (see "literacy goal setting" template at the end of chapter). The objectives stated the desired outcome, the personal reason for the objectives, and what specific steps the student planned to take in order to reach the concrete objective. For example:
   "My objective is to reach a _____ level (specify reading level) by (date). I want to do this because _____ (explain). I plan on achieving this goal by doing _____ (list steps that include concrete action and frequency)."In late February of the next calendar year, students revisited their goals, checked their achievement, and we then helped them to go through a guided reflection regarding their successes and any shortcoming they would list. They then wrote new goals for the conclusion of our research project in mid-April.
2. Background and Baseline Data:
   The targeted population was upper grades elementary students of Coronado Elementary School, which includes six classrooms from grades four to six. The actual participants were students in a 4th/5th grade combination class. The class consisted of seventeen 4th graders and sixteen 5th graders for a total of 33 students in the class. Students were selected to participate in the focus group based on their enrollment in one of the team member's 4th/5th combination class.
   Selection of participants followed convenience sampling, which is a nonprobability sampling method. Three students were newcomers to the country and were just beginning to learn English. Two others had Individualized Education Plans, and one had a special education plan. Comparative group students were enrolled in two 4th grade classes and one 5th grade class in the same school. In order to be part of the study, students

needed to be enrolled in one of our team member's classroom for the full academic year so that their initial and their April STAR Reading scores could be compared. Ultimately, one-fifth grade student was removed from this group for a final total of 32 students.

We created a pre- and post-survey for the four classrooms involved (focus group and control group) of fourth and fifth grade students using Google Forms. The team administered the pre-survey to students in mid-December—the baseline data—and the post-survey in late April—the comparative data set. The purpose of the survey was to determine if students experienced a shift of attitude or of perception about reading after setting objectives. We also wanted to watch said changes and compared them to their peers who did not set goals.

It is necessary to also note here that at our site all classroom teachers administered the STAR Reading assessment periodically throughout the school year, pre-determined by the district assessment calendar, a practice that contribute to the reports showing students' Grade Equivalency in their classes and each class overall. All classrooms used the same District approved curriculum. The collaborative research team compared the STAR Reading student data from September and our own survey results from December of the same year, to those collected in April of the following calendar year, to gauge changes. We entered each student's growth score from the Growth Report into an Excel spreadsheet and then applied the average formula to calculate a more precise class mean.

3. Material and Human Resources:

We count with the three members of our principal research team, the classrooms, and the materials normally assigned to our classrooms. We plan to maximize the use of Google docs and other internet resources available to the team through the school district. The school administration has given full support and will provide extra time for our data collection, analysis, and reports. Our research team will share the study findings in the first meeting at the start of the school year.

4. Theory of Action:

We conjectured the following:

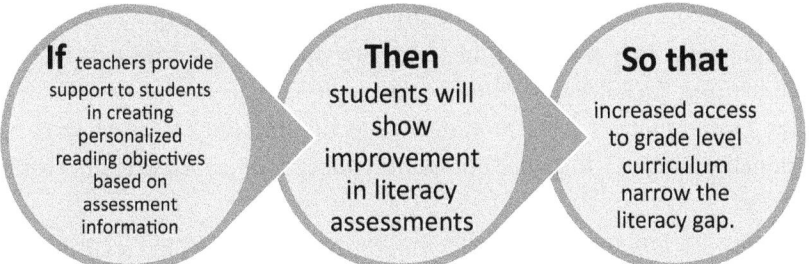

Figure 2.5: Our theory of action
Source: Marymor, Rivera & Walsh © 2018

Evidence

We understand evidence as an observable physical incidence, belief, or proposition, which can be corroborated. In other words, the preponderance of the evidence constitutes satisfactory grounds to conclude that a given occurrence (i.e., phenomenon) is true.

Evidence runs closely with claims. As we previously have said a claim, or a statement of truth, is always substantiated with evidence. We do claim what we can support with the evidence. The evidence shows that, indeed, what we state that exists does exist. When we assert the presence of a challenge, we immediately add the evidence supporting said assertion. The evidence glues our inductive research approach—from the ground up.

Collaborative action research, in other words, is about uncovering truths from the evidence we collect in the field. Evidence takes at least four forms—data, social consensus, expert opinion, and the knowledge available through the literature.

Data are contained in numbers and descriptions. Numbers usually are expressed through descriptive and inferential statistical measures. In a way, numbers represent reality in a compressed form. For instance, when we say that about one out of every four children in the country speak a language other than English, we are summarizing a huge amount of individuals in 1% point that only takes three symbols: 25%. But if we want to represent the human story behind these numbers, and capture the full range of experiences lived by that population, we will need to use narratives expressed in a myriad of ways, from monographies, stories, testimonials, and biographic accounts, whether in written text, sound, or film recordings.

While separating data into qualitative (narratives), and quantitative (numbers) expressions may be useful, in reality we can now quantify narratives. For instance, using digital applications, we can do a frequency analysis of words, phrases, even sentences. Moreover, data collection instruments, such as surveys, traditionally designed to collect numerical data, may contain items requiring narratives.

Social Consensus means implicit collective agreement. Certainly, people without necessarily getting together, end up agreeing on something they collectively share. As Krueger (1998) posits, social consensus means the similar thoughts, feelings, actions about an issue between us and those of others.

In education, for example, we may arguably state that a great challenge facing public schools is the growing opportunity gap between students from a low socioeconomic background and those from a more affluent socioeconomic background. We can also state that such gap tends to primarily affect minoritized groups. Regardless of distinctions, the assertion seems generally accepted among educators in the entire country, to the point that we, the general public, do not need to dig into the existing statistics to agree with this assertion.

Social consensus can also be used to claim false collective agreements. Too frequently we hear statements that use discreet pieces of data to claim general untruths. These typically use stem sentences like "People in this state believe that." "Everybody in the whole world agrees with …" "In this country no one doubts that …" "The latest poll shows that voters in the entire region support …" "It is well known that …"

The use of social consensus as evidentiary material may represent a challenge to the principal research team, since it manifests a subjective appreciation of reality. Subjectivity here suggests the analytical process that leads us to form our position about an issue. What we hear from others, what we know from experience, what we read and learn, inform and shape our subjective position about issues. That's how by the early 1990s smoking tobacco in public spaces was viewed as anti-social behavior in California, the first state to enact a legal ban on tobacco in 1995.

Expertise is the other type of evidence. Expert opinion emanates from the authority groups or individuals gain through the legitimization of knowledge, accumulated experience, or both. Legitimation runs through formal institutions of learning such as universities, colleges, institutes, and agencies. It is typically conveyed through official recognitions, such as titles, diplomas, and affiliation. When a medical doctor displays on her office's walls all her titles and diplomas, she is letting her patients know that all those institutions have recognized her expert opinion. The doctor is legitimated by the issuing institutions. So is a teaching or administrative credential, a Master's degree diploma, a Ph.D. title, or membership to a reputed agency or institution.

Accumulated experience makes a person an expert. Knowing by repeated practice certainly builds a person's expertise on a specific endeavor. Thus, a person who has taught all grade levels, from kindergarten to fifth—sometimes sixth—grade for a number of years, can be defined as an elementary school expert. This person's opinion on say, a literacy program for primary education, might be quite important to the decision-making process—adopt or reject such program. We can say that this expert's credibility is anchored on practice. Moreover, when a person has gained considerable expertise through sustained, long practice, as well as through legitimized knowledge, then her or his opinion's weight increases exponentially. Think of the elementary school teacher with a Master's degree on literacy.

Expert opinion presents less of a challenge as evidence than social consensus. We can collect it through all kinds of means, from surveys and interviews, to sound and video recordings. We encourage targeting these experts as much as possible while conducting research. In fact, expert opinion is a very common legal practice. In collaborative action research, selecting an expert needs to consider a few key areas: (a) legitimacy of credentials, (b) knowledge of the specific field being researched, (c) independence from the challenge so that to reduce bias and conflict of interest, (d) easy access to both the expert herself as well as to diverse data points. The latter may prove crucial to our efforts to corroborate the evidence. Accessing diverse data points makes it possible to double and triple check data's validity and reliability.

The Literature is the other source of evidence. The amassed knowledge—publications as text, sound, visuals, film, and other digital formats—is found in archived documents in libraries, data bases. Peer reviewed publications are one of the most potent parts of the literature. These publications were authorized by field scientists who subjected the material to a rigorous critique. Magazines, newsletters, bulletins, circulars, newspapers, may also be utilized to corroborate and extend the evidence, but only as a complementary material. Peer reviewed journals still hold the highest authority on a topic,

Peer reviewed literature comes in the form of empirical, and of theoretical studies. Empirical studies refer to research conducted within the physical world, and social organizations such as a school, a factory, a hospital, a neighborhood, or a county. Theoretical studies refer to research of existing studies and theoretical proposals in the field, with the purpose to advance new theories, perspectives, and positions on a concrete topic. These can also be meta-analysis—that is studies that bring together a set of studies to show the repeated patterns and the overarching truths. Consulting and using the empirical and theoretical research as evidence makes up the body of work captured in the literature review section of a research project. In Chapter Four we detail key aspects of the literature.

Now, let's visit another dimension of evidence—attribution, which is the constant purposeful analytical thinking we engage in our efforts to explain the reasons why events happen the way they do.

Attribution

Attribution plays a fundamental function in research, and in life generally. It runs tethered to the success or failure of an action, simply because we naturally seek to assign possible cause to all events. If we toss a coin into the air and see it coming down to the ground, we immediately attribute this fact to the pull of gravity, something we had no understanding until the seventeen hundreds. We always try to ascribe cause to every occurrence taking place around us, even if we do not rationally think that this is what we are doing, in that very instant. In other words, attribution is inherently linked to our lived experience.

For the purposes of this book we look at two kinds of attribution: intrinsic (endogenous), and extrinsic (exogenous).

Intrinsic Attribution: when we connect the outcomes of an action to our own individual or collective agency, and we clearly define the boundaries of responsibility to factors within, we can then say that we attribute the results of an action intrinsically. We, individually or as a collective, assume full responsibility for the results regardless of their nature. When endogenous attribution rules in an organization, learning is high—people build stronger sense of ownership of their actions, and it is predictable that they more easily will embrace corrective measures.

Intrinsic attribution suggests some degree of control of the possible factors that have created the issue. Within the confines of a school, for instance, learning and teaching sit at the core of its existence. Everything that occurs inside it revolves around said duty. Thus, students, teachers, administrators, custodians, service staff, and parents congregate around one purpose: advocate for students' learning. It is fair to assume then, that within this environment, a principal research team will have easy access to all these stakeholders, to the institution's data systems, and all other internally generated reports, studies, students' work.

Moreover, factors underpinning learning and teaching—such as setting reading objectives as the Marymor, Rivera & Walsh team did—reside right there, in the institution itself. Any action targeting root level factors can be launched, followed through, documented, and post-assessed.

Extrinsic Attribution: when we connect the outcomes of an action to factors outside of ourselves, as individual or as collective agents, we say that we assign accountability to extrinsic factors. We externalize responsibility. Locating the root-level factors outside the organization displaces our individual and collective obligations somewhere else, to a place and people we have little or no ways to affect said outcomes directly. When we place responsibility on exogenous factors, learning may not happen at all—people do not own their actions, and thus, corrective engagement may seem unnecessary.

In the case of the Marymor, Rivera & Walsh team presented above, we could have said that the significant improvement in reading may have been due to parental high-income background. The reasoning would go like this: Given that higher income level correlates with higher education attainment, it is very likely that parents, in this case, would have oriented their children in the use of their personal computers for learning purposes, and thus setting reading objectives was just normal.

While there might be some truth to the external role of parental influence in children's computer use, we need to carefully consider it as such—extrinsic factor. In other words, a principal research team ought to explore external factors as complementary to the internal ones. An analogy may be handy here: The researchers see everything through a bifocal pair of glasses.

The central focal lens considers all intrinsic factors as *determinant* forces of the issue under study, the locus of control resides inside the organization. The peripheral lens considers all extrinsic factors as *complementary* forces of the issue under study, but the locus of control still resides inside. Placing responsibility this way triggers a whole series of consequential pedagogical, social, and behavioral decisions that may render great benefits for all participants. But if intrinsic factors are considered isolated from its social, cultural, and economic context, the analysis will be faulty at best. The consequences may be detrimental.

In addition to assigning responsibility, attribution helps us to predict events. The results of the study conducted by the Marymor, Rivera & Walsh team showed that the action (teaching students to set reading objectives) produced important improvement among the participating children. It would not be too complicated to predict that if this support system were to be replicated with other children in similar conditions, it would create about the same or higher benefits; and if

64 | *Community-Owned Knowledge*

the support system were to be extended to the entire institution, the chances of overall, school-wide literacy improvement, could be significant.

Determining the intrinsic factors actually presents itself a challenge. Three activities typically take place during this phase of the research process.

(a) Upon close examination of all the evidence available, we first may narrow the scope of the issues to the most glaring and important. Here, a consensus building mechanism comes handy.
(b) Second, we bring to bear participants' accumulated expertise on the issues.
(c) Third, we consult the literature on the subject.

See illustration in Figure 2.6

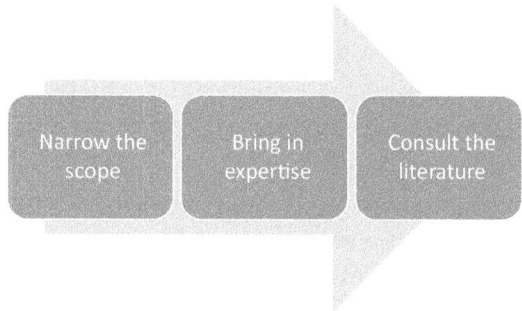

Figure 2.6: Locating intrinsic factors
Source G. Arriaza © 2020

And still we might not be as accurate. Deciding on the one factor in the realm of a human organization implies some degree of subjectivity. As suggested earlier, we bet on the lever we assume may produce the greatest impact and thus, provoke the changes we conjecture will be the most beneficial. Honing on in a concrete issue implies that we established attribution—we have concluded that by addressing and understanding such issue, we may produce change, institutional change.

Then we may be ready to say: we will focus our action research on this one issue. That's how the Marymor, Rivera, & Walsh team reached their conclusion on literacy as the challenge, and setting reading objectives as the action.

Fallacies

One more point to consider to establish attribution—the role of fallacies. For the purposes of this book we understand fallacy as faulty and misleading reasoning. Among some of the factors inducing faulty reasoning, fallacies perhaps exert the most influence. Similar to addressing our own biases, being aware of the most common fallacies, and being able to keep them at bay, may help us to improve the degree of accuracy when defining the challenge.

Here we list six popular ones:

Post Hoc: asserts that what happened right now is due to something that happened just before it. This fallacy enjoys popularity due to the fact that, many things happen in such close sequence, like when we hear a thunder in the sky and a few seconds later rain falls. But in most cases, especially within the social world, the fact that B happens after A does not mean A, caused B. For instance, students' algebra test results increased, in the aggregate, after a few hours of an intense classroom practice session on equations before the test. The Ad hoc fallacy attributes this pre-test practice as the cause of the improved results. While this pre-test practice may have something to do with the results, it does not account for the background knowledge students arrived at the pre-test activity with, their study habits, or that some of the students rehearsed test taking techniques before the pre-test practice. Additionally, if we disaggregate the data from the test, the results may show us a nuanced reality.

Ad Populum: an assertion is true because it is popular. Also known as the bandwagon fallacy, it wants us to rush our judgment to agree with what appears enjoying popularity. For instance,

> In a survey conducted in our site we found that 75% of adults agree with the proposition: 'when a rule is broken a swift disciplinary action must be taken'. The phrase 'swift disciplinary action' wants us to believe that most adults want the implementation of punitive actions every time a rule is broken.

But if the concepts "rule" and "disciplinary action" were further explored, perhaps the actions to be taken might not necessarily be punitive. Reality is way more complex than what ad populum fallacies advocate. Popularity does not make an assertion true.

Hasty Generalization: Typically, these generalizations are based on a conclusion emanating from insufficient evidence. For instance:

> In a study of a cohort of thirty freshmen it was found that students - regardless of gender, socioeconomic, ethnic, and friendship networks background 87 put in an average of two hours per homework assignment. Students at this institution are quite studious, and dedicated.

In this example, the author should have claimed that the freshmen cohort, and only that cohort, on the average exhibits a significant amount of time invested in homework assignments. No data were provided about the rest of the institution's students, and nothing about the qualities "studiousness" and "dedication." Again, disaggregating the overall results may portray the situation differently.

We can only claim what we research. Hasty generalizations only lead to error.

Ad Hominem: An assertion is rejected based on a critique to its proponent, and not on the merits of the assertion itself. This fallacy proposes that just because an individual promotes an argument, it must be dismissed, regardless of the degree of truthfulness of said proposition. Each source of our study's data must be taken with a degree of skepticism until corroborated through triangulation procedures, but this does not imply the automatic dismissal of data provided by an individual based on his or her character. Of course, if the data emanate from an individual widely known for unreliable, this person shouldn't have been, for instance, interviewed in the first place. For example:

> We cannot take into account the data produced by our interview of Dr. Siboney on the issue of bond-based financing, because she failed to report her center's funding in last year's report.

Rejecting data on financing because Dr. Siboney did not report the funding of her own center, whatever that may mean, seem farfetched, and incongruous with a study seeking to understand bond-based financing. Her failure at reporting the center's funding does not disqualify Dr. Siboney as someone who knows about finances.

Argument from Authority: whereas expert opinion may contribute to our understanding of an issue, we still must make sure that the expertise is actually on the subject matter being researched, but that it also counts as just one of the sources, and not the sole source. For instance: A study trying to understand how students with special needs fare in unrestricted environments at the classroom level, collected data from the water polo coach. The coach spends practically all her day in the swimming pool area. This source would not make much sense. But, interviewing a special education professional with classroom responsibilities does. The fallacy, in this case, wants us to consider attribution of expertise to any educator, regardless of the specificity of the issue being researched.

Red Herring: consists of an argument used to distract and divert attention from the main issue. For instance:

Researcher: "A spike in disciplinary actions issued to boys took place by the end of last quarter. What happened?"
School Vice-principal: "We have had some challenges, but we are committed to all students' safety. We promote both respect for each other and focused learning. Boys are not different than girls."

The researcher is asking concretely about the increased discipline actions dispensed to boys. The respondent, thinly acknowledged the issue, and immediately directed the researcher's attention to other less problematic climate issues. When interviewing, the researcher needs to keep close attention to distractions respondents may throw in the way, and avoid collecting useless data.

Key Chapter Learning

This chapter focuses on the crucial role of culture and structures play in our efforts to locate and define a challenge worth researching. Understanding our organization's culture and the ways it works underpins any attempt at addressing an issue affecting the organization's life, and its performance—e.g., teacher work satisfaction, parental involvement, student academics. We explained the function of collaborative action research as both a democratization force, and as an organizational learning strategy. In this sense, knowledge is horizontally shared and treated as common good. Moreover, the critical look into our own practices absorbs us all in a cycle of inquiry which, when reinforced throughout the organization's systems, becomes the most meaningful, and inexpensive professional learning development activity.

We also examined the crucial value of cultural habits. We outlined six core habits proven extremely successful in an organization's efforts to identify a challenge: do not jump to conclusions and solutions; try to explore root level factors; check evidence against the institution's vision and mission; remove impulse to blame and to feel guilty; base all discussion on the evidence available at the moment; analyze by prioritizing internal factors over external ones.

The chapter also explained the importance of situating the challenge within its academic, social, cultural, structural, and environmental context. While we need to narrow the challenge to its most concrete level, we need to also keep in mind its surrounding circumstances. As in the natural world, everything in a human organization is interconnected and functions interdependently. The chapter then describes how the challenge we have identified (the one we concluded that by acting on it we would transform our organization) is being dealt with by the organization. We called this "the action," to which we tied the functions that evidence and attribution play. We closed the chapter by visiting the potential perniciousness of faulty analysis, and warned us about fallacies, of which we listed some of the most popular in the research and education fields.

Essential Questions

How would you describe the culture of evidence examination at your institution? In what ways can you infuse collaborative action research into this culture?

Activity

1. Using the five whys (see resources below) first hone in on a challenge worth investigating at your institution. We highly recommend using actual data from your workplace. Go over at least one full set of the five whys.
2. Formulate a data statement.
3. Produce a research question (see Chapter Three and Five for more details on questions).
4. If you want to practice with artificial data, read first the case below, go over at least one full set of Five Whys, and do items 2 and 3 above.
5. Note that the team who wrote this brief report determined third grade as the focal issue. Explain your rationale if, after your first round of Five Whys, you concluded that it is not the third grade where the challenge resides. Formulate what the focal issue is for you (your team).

Lincoln Elementary School Case[1]

A five-year old census shows the school student population as 70% Latino/a, 20% White non-Hispanic, and 10% Asian (Korean, Chinese); Dual English

---

1 All names are pseudonyms. Ethnic and racial labels were kept as they appeared in the original school report.

Language Learners 40% (Spanish, Korean, Mandarin). The school is located in an affluent neighborhood of Coppercorn, a midsize city in Nowhere. The school became a conversion charter after parents from the Latinx community organized and petitioned the district for charter approval. From a 70% Latinx student body, over the last two years there has been an increasing influx of White Non-Hispanic, Chinese and Korean children. The school's demographics changed along with housing around the site. The median price of a family house varies from $900 thousand to one million and a half US Dollars. Today, the school student demographics show the following: 30% Mexican, non-White Hispanic; 20% White, non-Hispanic; 50% Asian (Korean and Chinese American).

Lincoln Elementary has been in Program Improvement (PI) status since the 2017–2018 school year. According to the Accountability Report (AR) of the Academic Performance Index (API), the school is listed in the third year as its PI status. As the No Child Left Behind Act of 2001 has faded away, a new testing accountability system has fully began. As the following graph shows, 55% of the third graders at the school have not met the standards for English language arts test. An additional 41% of third graders nearly met the standard, so that equates to only 14% of third graders having met or exceeded the standards in language arts. According to the Nowhere Department of Education (NDE) website test results, only 25% of third graders district-wide in Coppercorn City are reading at grade level. In comparison, statewide, 38% of students in third grade met or exceeded standard in English language arts/literacy.

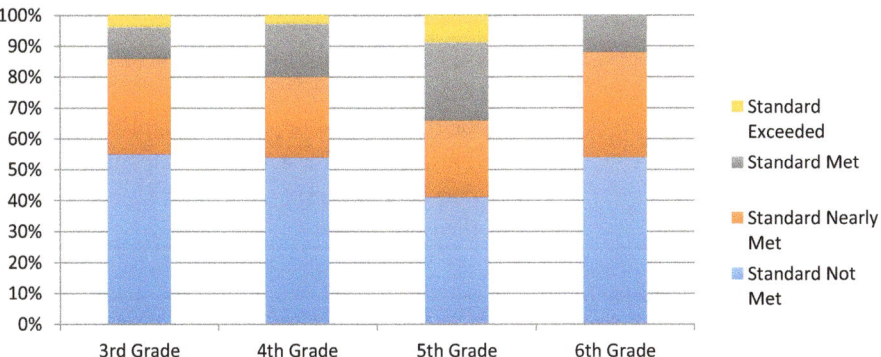

Figure 2.7: English language arts/literacy achievement level distribution
Source: Nowhere, Lincoln Elementary, Department of Education (NDE) Website.

Resources

Growing Social Capital in the Classroom by Arriaza, G., & Rocha, C. (Spring, 2016). https://files.eric.ed.gov/fulltext/EJ1100297.pdf

Minnesota Department of Education: Root Cause Analysis Protocol—Fish bone https://www.spps.org/site/handlers/filedownload.ashx?moduleinstanceid=59054&dataid=61130&FileName=Fishbone%20for%20Root%20Cause.pdf

National School Reform Faculty: The five whys https://www.nsrfharmony.org/wp-content/uploads/2017/10/5_whys_0.pdf

Invista Performance Solutions
www.invistaperforms.org

Intervention Organizer Template

1. Issue	Succinctly describes the challenge the action attempts to address: the issue, the evidence, and the concern it raises.
2. Goals and objectives	Lists goals and specific objectives the action tries to accomplish, including the action's timeline.
3. Nature of intervention	Describes the central components of the action, and the steps or phases it follows.
4. Resources	List the amount of money, type of materials, and the people needed to implement and to sustain the intervention. Include, if needed, role of the school administration and role of district central office.
5. Signposts (indicators)	Identify and explain the indicators (qualitative and/or qualitative baseline data) that will be followed throughout the intervention.
6. Participants	Describe the targeted population. Explain selection criteria and profile actual participants.
7. Theory of action	Formulate proposition: If . . . then . . . so that . . .

Student Literacy Objective Setting

Objectives
My first objective is to (explain) I want to accomplish my objective by (set dates) I have this objective because (explain) I plan on achieving this objective by taking these actions (list)

Objectives
My second objective is to (explain)   I want to accomplish my objective by (set dates)   I have this objective because (explain)   I plan on achieving this objective by taking these actions (list)
My third objective is to (explain)   I want to accomplish my objective by (set dates)   I have this objective because (explain)   I plan on achieving this objective by taking these actions (list)

References

Argyris, C. (1977). Organizational learning and management information systems. *Database for Advances in Information Systems* (winter-spring), (13) 2-3, 3-11

Argyris, C. (2002). Double loop learning. Teaching, and research. *Academy of Management Learning, and Education, 1*(2), 206–218.

Habermas, J. (1998). *The theory of communicative action* (Vol. I e II). Cambridge, UK: Polity Press.

Henze, R. C., Katz, A., Norte, E., & Sather, S. (2001). *Leading for diversity: How school leaders can improve interethnic relations.* Center for Research on Education Diversity & Excellence. Washington, DC.

Kandel, E. R. (2007). *In search of memory. The emergence of a new science of mind.* New York, NY: W.W. Norton and Co. Inc.

Krueger, J. (1998). On the perception of social consensus. *Advances in Experimental Social Psychology*, 30, 163–240.

3

The Question

We, at Bayview Elementary School, agreed that even though students came from a rich diversity of socio-economic, ethnic, and multilingual backgrounds, they were not realizing their potential by being placed in segregated classrooms. It appeared to us that our low performing school was unable to capitalize on the knowledge that students brought from their homes to promote student academic success. Locked in a traditional institution, bilingual and monolingual learners were segregated, and single-aged graded classrooms were the norm.

With the encouragement of colleagues, parents, and administrators, four of us piloted a team taught, multi-aged dual language program for a cross-section of the school's 5–7-year-olds. We, as teachers, had experienced several years of segregation with bilingual learners in a track, monolingual English speakers in another, and students in Special Education classes in yet another track. Possibilities for students to change tracks from a low-demanding academics to one of high-demanding academics were limited, and interactions among students from various tracks were minimal.

The great challenge that we faced was the school's tracking policy of linguistic segregation by classroom which hindered meaningful opportunities for English learners to interact in classrooms with diverse English-speaking peers. Likewise, all students had limited contact with the rich cultural and linguistic heritages on the school campus. Challenging the tracking policy, in order to restructure the traditional institution through the pilot-study, offered the opportunity to expand the pilot school-wide in the coming years.

Leo Sheejan, Bayview teacher

The Research Question

The *question* asked in a collaborative action research project, first and foremost, is one that participants are interested in and are concerned with. The question stems directly from the identified challenge (the details of which we discussed in Chapter Two) focusing on an issue of practice that is not overly broad or theoretical but intersects with theory. In a sense, the research question synthesizes the challenge and guides entirely our research project. It uncovers answers that enhance our understanding.

> **STEP ONE:**
>
> **FORMULATE A RESEARCH QUESTION**

A research team brainstorms possible questions that are representative of the challenge and considers again and again what is known about the challenge until the team agrees on the question closest to the challenge. By representative we mean how closely the question mirrors and summarizes the challenge we have identified and defined. The production of a research question, therefore, offers an opportunity for a team to deepen the understanding of the challenge, to learn from each other, and to build their work experience as a team, in short, to grow their professional capacity.

At each step in the creation of the research question, the research team needs a well-facilitated process, which may take the following steps:

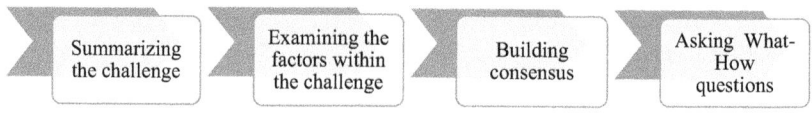

Figure 3.1: Research question creation process
Source: G. Arriaza and L. Scott © 2020

Summarizing the Challenge

Initially, there must be an open discussion based on a succinct definition of the challenge. As we explained in Chapter Two, such definition must include the data substantiating it. For instance, the principal research team of Bayview Elementary School from our vignette above had gained agreement on a significant area for investigation, as they assert: The school's tracking policy of linguistic segregation by classroom hindered meaningful opportunities for English learners to interact in classrooms with diverse English-speaking peers.

They also concluded that the challenge consisted of the absence of the promotion of an asset-based approach to schooling.

Examining the Factors within the Challenge
Next, the research team must look closely at the factors within the challenge to determine whether the research question has the potential to lead to further discovery. In the words of Krathwohl, "Clearly, some questions lend themselves to investigation more than others" (2009, p. 196).

In our example, the team identified these factors: linguistic, socioeconomic, ethnic, and cross-age interactions; academic success; and social-emotional learning (SEL). Teachers looked at the low performance of many students and the lack of student interaction across linguistic tracks. They closely examined the limited amount of high-demanding academic activities in some tracks and students' limited contact with the rich cultural and linguistic heritages across the entire school campus.

As the research team considered the research question, they examined their potential to investigate student interactions, activities, and their access to academic and social emotional information that would be pertinent to answering the question.

Building Consensus
Coming down with agreements within the research team assures that there is shared concern and understanding of the challenge and agreement that the research question can guide a fruitful investigation of the issues at hand. At Bayview, teachers achieved an important consensus when they agreed to examine the impacts of the tracks' constraint of student interactions.

Consensus does not mean 100% agreement by the research team members, reaching consensus rather means that the research team is on the same page and is willing to move toward an understanding that works for everyone. Hence, building a consensus engages all team members inclusively, so that the team is empowered to move forward.

Asking What-How Questions
Finally, when formulating the research question, the research team poses a *What-How* type of question. The team at Bayview asked: In what ways might restructuring the school for linguistic, socioeconomic, ethnic, and cross-age interactions impact academic success and social-emotional learning (SEL)? Posing such a

question is not only useful in gathering information and problem solving, but it also guides discovery of *what* the needed input might be (e.g., restructuring the school for various interactions) and *how* this input may impact the desired output (e.g., greater academic success and SEL). Asking *What-How* types of questions has the potential to create new areas of thinking and uncover new information.

Indeed, asking questions is a magnificent trait of our species. We ask questions in search of answers and, that way, for a moment to fulfill our ignorance; new questions emerge with every response we create. We pose them to think deeply about a topic, the unknown. Curiosity causes us to spend time and energy acquiring knowledge to solve what may be mysterious, address a concrete need, or to just enjoy it. Whether we articulate our questions or not, it seems that we devote considerable amounts of our brainpower seeking an answer to them, and thus building knowledge and understanding. It has been said that the core function of our human brain is to learn.

In order to learn, we—whether as teachers, or as students—ask questions much like eternal innovators fidgeting with the limits of our imagination, in search of solutions, responses to what challenges or intrigues us. Educators are the ultimate creators; their function is to always ask students questions to determine what they know and to push them to unsuspected worlds. In the realm of natural and social sciences, asking the right question may lead to crucial discoveries, to ignite new perspectives in our understanding of phenomena, and to reduce our state of confusion.

For the research team to gain new perspectives in search of answers they need meaningful research questions which they cannot answer with the current knowledge they possess (Sagor, 1997). Any given day we are inundated by countless learning and teaching experiences. Finding the best moment to challenge students with a new idea, re-teach a concept that has not been fully understood, or select lessons that will engage a particular group of students are all instances that would be worthy of reflection and study, yet not all these concerns become a research project, nor they should necessarily become one.

As we noted above, wrestling with the articulation of the research question implicates a very intentional learning process. Research questions are about deliberate inquiry, and collaborative action research offers participants an environment of constant checking in to reflect and compare their thoughts in an ongoing basis. We learn and grow to greater understanding when we first define a challenge (as we presented in Chapter Two) and then when we pose a research question. Said learning enables us, as individuals and as collectives, to build higher degrees of professional and technical capacity, which over time translates into our institutions' intelligence—local research capacity equals greater organizational capacity. And as we have stated before, we formulate a research question on the assumption that by better understanding the challenge, the better equipped we are to enact transformational change in our institutions.

Figure 3.2: Research question (birds-eye view) components at ground level

The research question is the synthesis of the challenge in front of us. From a birds-eye view, this type of question guides a whole research effort, therefore, it is always high up looking down at the ground. Like a lighthouse beacon, it keeps our attention gravitating toward its concrete and precise direction; but it alone cannot be directly answered (see Figure 3.2.). In order to find the responses to such question, we need to carefully follow a series of steps to find ways to investigate and examine its core components at the ground level.

Thus, before we launch an effort to find responses to the Bayview teacher's research question—In what ways might restructuring the school for linguistic, socioeconomic, ethnic, and cross-age interactions impact academic success and social-emotional learning?—we need to find ways, at the ground level, to examine its core components, hereafter called variables, factors, and items. In other words, we must determine how these components may express themselves in real time, before our own very eyes. We call *operationalizing the question* to this process

Operationalizing of the Research Question

Operationalizing the research question into its various parts begins with carefully considering its input and output components. A research question contains at least two variables, one that exists on its own and varies independently, which we call independent or input, and another that depends on the first one,

78 | *Community-Owned Knowledge*

which we call dependent or output. Like the case of a person who goes to the physician complaining about hair loss. The physician prescribes a successful shampoo to address immediately. In this case, the shampoo would be the input side, or independent variable, and the stop of hair loss the output, or dependent variable.

Once we identify the variables of our research question then we can look for the other two major components: the factors within each variable, and the items that make up each factor (see Figure 3.3).

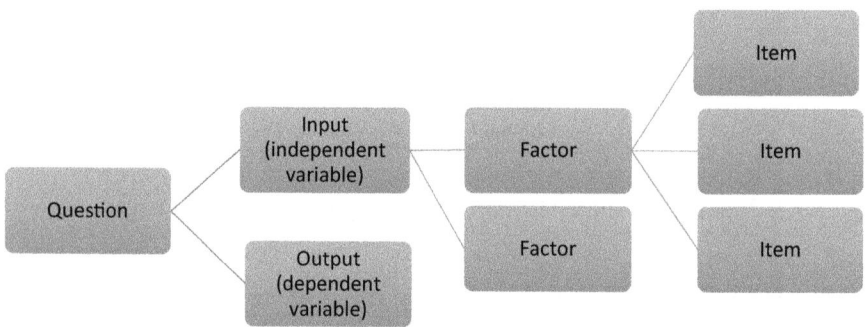

Figure 3.3: Operationalizing the question
Source: G. Arriaza and L. Scott © 2020

For example, the principal research team at Bayview conjectured that linguistic, socioeconomic, ethnic, and cross-age interactions may improve students' academic success and SEL. This assumption distills the team's discussions about what they considered the challenge. Their efforts to frame the challenge in a meaningful and clear way, facilitated their own understanding of the complexities of the challenge itself. The question, again, was this:

> In what ways might restructuring the school for linguistic, socioeconomic, ethnic, and cross-age interactions impact academic success and social-emotional learning?

At the heart of their research question we find two variables:

1. the structure for student interactions, and
2. the students' academic performance and social-emotional learning.

Restructuring the school for linguistic, socioeconomic, ethnic, and cross-age interactions is the input that the team envisions as operating independently and having an impact on student outcomes. Improved student academic performance and SEL—the output which depend on the restructuring.

> **STEP TWO:**
>
> **BREAK THE RESEARCH QUESTION INTO ITS COMPONENTS:**
>
> A. INPUT—Independent Component
> B. OUTPUT—Dependent Component

Variables

First, let's work with the input side: restructuring the school's interactions. In this variable resides the school's policy of tracking students by four dimensions: linguistic, socioeconomic, ethnic, and cross-age. These are the conditions in which students learn and teachers work regardless of the impact on students' academic performance or SEL.

Second, we now need to work with the output side: The student outcomes come into our view as the other component. The principal research team speculated that the Bayview students would experience improved outcomes along two dimensions: academic success and enhanced SEL. This would be the result or output of restructuring. Thus, according to this assumption students' academic success and SEL was dependent on the restructuring of school's interactions along the lines of four dimensions: linguistic, socioeconomic, ethnic, and cross-age. The team would need to identify ways at the ground level to investigate these dimensions and their impact on students' academic performance and SEL in order to find answers about how restructuring might benefit students.

Factors

Now, let's look at the factors embedded in each of these two variables. Factors are the categories at each variable's core that might be a fact, a circumstance, or an influence, contributing to an outcome or result. At Bayview the team envisioned the structure of interactions as the one factor on the input side that functioned independently of other factors. Thus, restructuring might impact the two factors of academic performance and SEL on the output side that are dependent on the structure of the interactions at the school.

> **STEP THREE:**
>
> **TAKE COMPONENTS ONE AT A TIME, AND BREAK THEM INTO FACTORS:**
> *Note: For brevity purposes we will look only at one factor in the input and one in the output components. Here we will also identify the core components for each of the factors.*
>
> A. INDEPENDENT
>   1. STRUCTURE OF INTERACTIONS
>
> B. DEPENDENT
>   1. ACADEMIC PERFORMANCE
>   2. SOCIAL-EMOTIONAL LEARNING

All three factors, restructuring, academic performance, and SEL, are essential aspects of the aboveground, overview of the school. Examining them closely aids our effort to get as near as possible to a ground-level position. However in order to get here, we need to break each factor down further to determine the concrete expressions of each in a real time, actual daily experience. This step is called itemizing.

Items

Finally, we need to examine the concrete forms in which a factor manifests itself in day-to-day experiences. The principal research team could potentially examine each of the factors stated above and get as close to a granular level as they can through each successive itemization. When itemizing, we seek to identify, to the best of our knowledge, the indicators that tell us when and how the issue we investigate manifests in day-to-day reality. It also defines the most basic components of the research question.

> **STEP FOUR:**
>
> **BREAK FACTORS INTO ITEMS.**
> *Note: For space reasons we only will break down one factor into smaller units here.*
>
> A. INDEPENDENT
>   1. STRUCTURE OF INTERACTIONS
>   a) LINGUISTIC
>   b) SOCIOECONOMIC
>   c) ETHNICITY, AND
>   d) AGE OR GRADE

For space reasons we will only work with one of the input factors here: *Structure of Interactions*. The structure of the school's interactions can be itemized along the lines of four dimensions: linguistic, socioeconomic, ethnic, and age or grade.

The research team identified the segregation of the classrooms by students' home languages as the first item needed in the restructuring process. This item can be further broken down by language, English or Spanish, and closer to the ground level, we can itemize the languages spoken by the teachers and assistants, the languages present in the school curriculum, and the languages used by the students in their day-to-day interactions.

At this point we need to consider real-life issues that we can break down, as close to a granular level as possible, and that determined the students' daily interactions. For example, Bayview's physical school building had 14 self-contained classrooms which could accommodate up to 30 students each. Fourteen credentialed teachers taught at the school along with various support and administrative personnel. Each classroom had student and teacher furniture and developmentally appropriate teaching resources.

We can also consider the state-approved curriculum and assessment plan provided by the district. From this detailed level we can construct instruments, such as a rubric or a questionnaire, which will ultimately guide our data collection work. Check Chapter Five for details on this point.

With the various components of the research question itemized, we next consider the formulation and design of our questions.

Question Design

Each step of our question design brings the research question closer to the ground level (see Figure 3.4.). Once we have itemized the question's factors, we may be ready to formulate our questions. In order to do we must be sure that we can define, operationalize, measure, and build both reliability and validity throughout the questions. This action will increase the possibility that our research question guides meaningful inquiry.

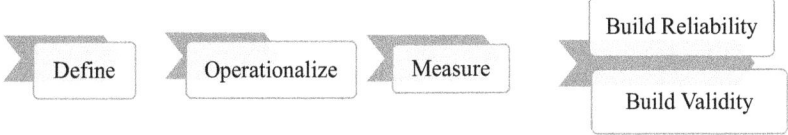

Figure 3.4: Question design steps
Source: G. Arriaza and L. Scott © 2020

Define the Question

This means that the principal research team facilitates understanding of what each item signifies in real time, real life. The team establishes an agreed upon meaning for the various concepts, terms, and abstractions. They define what is meant by school or academic success, or conceptually, what is meant by cultural awareness through interactions.

For example, to define academic success the Bayview teachers started with the current definition from the school policy, which used standardized test scores and grades on progress reports. Next, the team considered how students might demonstrate academic success in ways that were not captured by their standardized test scores, grades, or other summative assessments. They discussed the need to include student reflections about their own growth, as shown in portfolios, and teachers' anecdotal notes and interview responses. Finally, the team sought consensus on a shared definition of academic success. At each point in the team's deliberation, they evaluated existing definitions and proposed refinements to guide their question design.

For instance, when they discussed the term academic success the team looked for student work to substantiate improvement over time. They reviewed writing samples in student portfolios which had been selected by the student and the teacher and scored on a rubric. They triangulated these scores with standardized test scores of writing and student grades on progress reports. In this way the team agreed that academic success in writing was multi-dimensional.

Operationalize the Question

After achieving consensus on the meaning of terms and concepts, we move to explain the steps or process needed to answer questions in a systematic way. Having a clear set of instructions to present and measure the items within the research question ensures consistency across comparable situations.

For example, to operationalize students' academic success the team at Bayview collected standardized test scores, grades, and portfolio data. They created rubrics to measure student improvement, and they returned to their definition of academic success to consider if teachers' anecdotal comments regarding academic growth on progress reports might fall within the definition. While examining the available existing data points in the language and literacy assessment data, they determined that both rubric data for writing portfolios and standardized measures for English language development, reading, and writing fit in the definition of academic success and would thus be included in answering the question. Because the team speculated that academic performance would improve with restructuring, at each step they needed to select the sources of available assessment data that would best capture what they had intended in their agreed upon definition.

Measure the Question

Measuring is quantifying two or more characteristics, objects, or events so that they can be compared and measured. Not all human experience can be measured. How do we measure subjective factors such as *efficacy* or *grit*? According to Bandura (1993), when we do measure subjective factors, it is an act that reflects an individual's own assumptions of said measurement. For instance, when we pose the question: on a scale of 1 (*weak*) to 3 (*strong*), how much grit does a specific student have? We arbitrarily decide what a 3 is from our own perception of *strong*.

Thus, at each stop of our systematic process, we confirm measurable data points aligned with each of our question's basic components.

For example, the team agreed that a standardized measure of writing achievement would be too narrow of a representation of academic success, so they included the writing portfolio and its rubrics as measurable data points. Teachers designed the writing rubrics and criterion, to capture a dimension of academic achievement in literacy which would complement the standardized assessments. They developed the rubric (see Table 3.1) for use with Spanish or English student writing samples.

Table 3.1: Writing Rubric (Ages 8–10)

Score	3	2	1
Content	Developed theme Specific details Relevant conclusion	Theme lacks some clarity General details Simple conclusion	Incoherent theme One or no detail No conclusion
Organization	Follows logical purpose Effective connections between ideas Consistent transitions	Mostly logical purpose Some connections present between ideas Transitions inconsistent at times	Does not follow logical purpose No connection between ideas Inconsistent transitions
Mechanics	Almost no spelling, grammar, or punctuation errors	Some spelling, grammar, or punctuation errors	Many spelling, grammar, or punctuation errors

Source: G. Arriaza and L. Scott © 2020

Build Reliability in a Question

Selecting measures in the question design that are consistent across comparable situations assures that we can use the instruments throughout the study. This also assures that we can use the instruments selected elsewhere under a similar context or circumstances and produce the same or similar result.

The principal research team uses the same type of measures for the same ground-level items across all of the instruments. They then look for patterns and regularity in their everyday observations and data collection.

For example, they examined historical data from standardized assessments to find whether student academic achievement within each segregated track had followed a similar pattern and whether new patterns might emerge in the new school configuration. By having consistent measures they were able to meaningfully compare academic performance across time periods and assure that under similar circumstances academic achievement would remain consistent.

In addition to asking what the writing rubric scores are in October and April each year, the team asked the following questions about academic performance in literacy or biliteracy for each student:

What is their developmental level in spelling in English? Spanish?
What texts are noted on the reading interests' survey?
What is their independent reading level?

They also asked questions about academic performance in math.

Build Validity in a Question

Valid question design occurs when the question measures what it intends to measure. In collaborative action research valid question design also requires that responses to questions mean the same to all principal research team members. The team may emphasize their efforts to build validity by working to eliminate ambiguity in their questions and collect answers that correspond to what they are intended to measure.

When we use multiple data points to confirm the same understanding, this further validates the question and data. This is a good way to *triangulate*. Triangulation of the data, as we further explain in Chapter Five, occurs when at least three points of inquiry measure the same item with the same results. When several assessments provide the same result, or differently worded questions elicit similar responses, the greater the validation.

For example, the Bayview teachers proposed looking at student academic success through both student and teacher reflection on the writing portfolios. The team triangulated the academic achievement literacy data by using the standardized writing scores as one; measurement of academic achievement, student self-evaluation rubric scores, and comments as another; and rubric scores and interview responses from teachers as a third. These routine steps at the ground level assured consistency, reliability, and validity.

The core ideas that we have presented in the question design include defining, operationalizing, measuring, and building reliability and validity in our questions. We now consider the types of questions that we ask at the ground level of our study.

Questions at the Ground Level

After making sure itemizing factors have been exhausted, we take one factor at a time and make every single item into a question at the ground level. In a sense they embody the ways the issue we want to study materializes in real time.

Questions can be either of two types: objective or subjective. Objective questions ask for factual information or responses that leave no room for opinion or interpretation. The response stems from straightforward logic and the answer remains the same regardless of the respondent. Subjective questions, on the other hand, ask for the attitude or opinion of the respondent and seek a value that may vary from person-to-person.

STEP FIVE: MAKE EVERY ITEM INTO A QUESTION

Once we determine if we want factual information or subjective values, we can formulate each question to solicit responses in one of two ways—closed and open-ended questions.

Closed questions are those where the answer is controlled by the interviewer. Respondents are given specific choices as responses. Yes/No questions are examples of closed responses to questions as are multiple choices or Likert scale responses.

For instance, in a scale of one: weak, two: satisfactory, three: strong, mark an X on one number only to the following:

(a) This student's cross-cultural awareness is:
   1. Weak
   2. Satisfactory
   3. Strong
(b) This student's social-emotional learning is:
   1. Weak
   2. Satisfactory
   3. Strong
(c) In this school the professional development is:
   1. Weak
   2. Satisfactory
   3. Strong

Open-ended questions are those where the answer is controlled by the interviewee. For instance:

> In what ways have the students demonstrated their academic achievement this year?
> Or,
> In what ways do these examples of writing in the portfolio show the student's best work?

Once we have our questions we put them all into a research instrument, such as a questionnaire guide in preparation for collecting data. Before we move on in the creation of the instruments to do the research let us show a summary of the five steps that underlie the whole process.

> First, formulate a research question.
> Second, break the research question into its independent and dependent components; the input that operates independently, and the output that is dependent.
> Third, take the components of the research question one at a time, and break them into factors.
> Fourth, break down each of the factors into smaller units or items.
> Finally, make every item into a question.

As we formulate our questions at the ground level, keep in mind the following issues, which we need to avoid.

Ten Pitfalls to Avoid in Formulating Questions

Besides being culturally and linguistically responsive to the participants, a series of precautions need to be taken care of when formulating our ground-level questions.

Here we list ten essential tips:

1. Avoid leading questions.
   Example:
   So, you agree with asking children to memorize text?
   Vs.
   What is your take on asking children to memorize text?
2. Avoid negative and positive associations.
   Example:
   How similar are your views on differentiation to constructivist teaching?
   Vs.
   What is your view on differentiated teaching? Now tell me what is your view on constructivist teaching?
3. Avoid negatively worded questions.
   Example:
   How come you don't agree with "packaged solutions" approaches?
   Vs.

How do you explain your position about "packaged solutions" approaches?
4. Use understandable, non-jargon language.
   Example:
   How do the Writing Assessment data results support your work at home helping your child's language acquisition and essay composition?
   Vs.
   How does the information of the high school exit exam help you support your child's language needs, such as speaking, and formal writing?
5. Avoid double-barrel questions.
   Example:
   Does your district have a policy that supports accountability and invests in accountability systems?
   Vs.
   What policies does your district have about accountability? Now tell me How about policies dealing with accountability systems?
6. Avoid asking the performance of several tasks.
   Example:
   First select the best three reading programs. Then Mark the one you prefer, and explain the reasons in this x black paper provided.
   Vs.
   I will ask you to do three sequential actions. Let's start.One, select the best three reading programs from this list (show list).Thanks. Now:Two. Mark from these three the one you prefer.Great. This is our final step: Explain to me the reasons you chose this program.
7. Do not use dichotomous questions.
   Example:
   Do you think distributive leadership improves student academic performance?
   Vs.
   To the best of your knowledge, how does distributive leadership affect student academic performance?
8. Do not ask questions inquiring something uncomfortable to answer (too personal) or about something the respondent perceives that the researcher wishes to have an answer in a particular way.
   Example:
   How is your current income affecting transportation or meals for your child?
   Vs.
   How is transportation working for your child so far?How has the cafeteria services experience for your child been this year?

9. Avoid asking too many open-ended questions. Try to use more closed questions to control the range of answers.
Example:
How has your child's experience in the school yard been recently?
Vs.
Circle one number. In a scale 1(unpleasant), 2 (somewhat pleasant), and 3 (pleasant), rank your child's experience so far at the school's year.
10. Almost all "why" questions pose problems because (a) these usually ask for causal relations, and (b) there is no frame of reference.
Example:
Why do you think students at this site do not place used paper in the recycle bin?
Vs.
What incentives does the school offer for recycling paper?

Key Chapter Learning

This chapter focuses on formulating and operationalizing the research question and understanding Question Design. Our first step is to formulate a research question which guides our collaborative action research by synthesizing the challenge we have identified. The research team brainstorms possible questions and agrees on the question closest to the challenge. This open discussion involves summarizing the challenge, examining the factors within the challenge, building consensus, and asking *What-How* questions. To determine whether the research question has the potential to lead to further discovery we examine the factors within the challenge. In building consensus we assure that our research question can guide a meaningful investigation and that we can find answers beyond our current knowledge.

The research question guides our whole research effort from a birds-eye view that is high up looking down. The research question cannot be directly answered, but we can operationalize it in order to investigate and examine its core components at the ground level in real time before our very own eyes. Breaking the research question into its various input and output components is our second step. The research question contains at least two variables, one that exists on its own that we call the independent variable or input, and another variable that depends on the first one that we call the dependent variable or output.

After identifying these variables our third step is to break them down further into what we call factors within each variable. Factors are the categories at each variable's core that might be a fact, a circumstance, or an influence, contributing to an outcome or result. Repeating this decomposition process, our fourth step is to break down each factor into items. Items are the concrete expressions of each factor in actual daily experiences. Our research team can continue this process, known as itemization, repeatedly. Each successive itemization gets us as close to a granular level where we can identify the indicators that tell us when and how the issue at hand manifests itself in day-to-day reality.

Question Design guides our fifth step when we make every item into a question. We must be sure that we can define, operationalize, measure, and build both reliability and validity throughout our questions in order to guide meaningful inquiry. Defining the question means that the team establishes an agreed upon meaning for various concepts, terms, and abstractions. Operationalizing means having a clear set of instructions to answer questions to ensure consistency across comparable situations. Measuring the question is quantifying characteristics, objects, or events so that they can be compared and measured. Building reliability and validity in a question means that the question design is consistent across comparable situations throughout the study and that the question measures what it intends to measure.

Finally, in making every item into a question at the ground level, the issue that we want to study materializes in real time. Our questions can be objective questions that ask for factual information that are not open to interpretation or opinion, or they can be subjective questions that seek a value that may vary from person-to-person or ask for an attitude or opinion of a respondent. Each question of the questions can be formulated as closed questions where the answer is controlled by the interviewer or open-ended questions where the answer is controlled by the interviewee.

Essential Questions

How will we operationalize the research question into its various components?
In what ways will our team define, operationalize, measure, and build both reliability and validity throughout our questions in order to guide meaningful inquiry?

90 | *Community-Owned Knowledge*

Activity

Read the brief case below of a principal research team. Next, follow the process for creating a research question (Figure 3.1) and operationalizing the question.

1. Consider what is known about the challenge, and define the challenge.
2. Brainstorm possible research question(s) representative of the challenge, and then determine the research question(s) closest to the challenge.
3. Operationalize the research question(s) into its variables, factors, and items. Note: For this activity break one variable into factors and one factor into items.

Parker High School Case

Students at Parker High are closely following media reports of police brutality and are motivated to take action in the local community. Students have asked teachers for more learning experiences related to the social justice movement, Black Lives Matter, and Say Her Name. For example, their English teacher, Ms. Treasure, is teaching them to work collaboratively and purposely to research the school and community's current response and connect this with historical events. She has asked them to consider what they hope to learn from their research and how they intend to use what they learn to help teach others, including their teachers.

Teachers at the high school recognize that students learn best when they are deeply engaged in the issues at hand. Teachers are also aware that their students' lived experience may be very different than their own. They are concerned that they must cover the school-approved curriculum without disrupting the learning of others or the work of other school staff.

Ms. Treasure let the students know that she is not very well versed in all of these topics. So they need to consider how to relate ideas to others who may have no idea what they are talking about. "And they're going to have to provide me with the research" (Personal communication, May 21, 2020). The students did the research and found articles online related to the issue nationally and in the community. They decided to interview the school security guard and the principal for their report and both are agreeable. One of the students reached out to the city police department and interviewed one of the officers about how they are handling the Black Lives Matter movement and how the department responded to an officer involved shooting where a Black man died. The man was the uncle to a classmate at the school and there was a lot of upheaval about it; something that the students are extremely passionate about.

Ms. Treasure told the students to "try to ask as many questions as possible and make sure that they get all of the information possible and look at both sides of it because they do have to have a counter argument in their essay when they turn it in. So they do have to look at both sides of the issue and be able to prove why they feel the way that they feel about this particular issue" (Personal communication, May 21, 2020).

Resources

Rothstein, D., & Santana, L. (2011). *Make just one change: Teach students to ask their own questions.* Cambridge, MA: Harvard Education Press.

LeCompte, M. D., & Schensul, J. J. (2010). *Designing and conducting ethnographic research: An introduction* (Vol. 1). Lanham, MD: Rowman Altamira.

Survey monkey (www.surveymonkey.com).

YouTube. Formulating a Research Question (www.youtube.com/watch?v=89NonP_iZZo) (https://www.youtube.com/watch?v=71-GucBaM8U)

References

Krathwohl, D. R. (2009). *Methods of educational and social science research: The logic of methods* (3rd ed.). Long Grove, IL: Waveland Press.

Sagor, R. (1997). Collaborative action research for educational change. *Association for Supervision and Curriculum Development-Yearbook*, 169–191.

4

What Is Known and What Is Possible

Looking at the background research we all chose to read two to three articles about our topic, school dress codes. To find public published sources, the university library has access to a large database of articles so that is where we started. There are search bars and we each used different keywords that had to do with our research question and saw what we could come up with the search engine.

I read about a case that went to the Supreme Court about students wearing armbands in some sort of protest. The school was trying to say that the students could not wear the armbands, and then it went to the Supreme Court that decided that the students were protected by the First Amendment. This decision brought into the conversation the idea of what role does the public school system have in saying what students can and cannot wear?

I was actually very curious about news articles too because dress code is something that is a contemporary topic that people are talking about now. So when I was looking at the history of it I used journal articles, but to see what school districts are doing right now, I used articles from news outlets in the area.

Also, reading the dress code policies of districts or schools that had a written dress code policy was one of the most interesting things that we compared because one school's dress code policy was really specific and others were very broad and generic. When one looks at the history of school dress codes, it is impossible not to take notice of the inconsistencies in policy, philosophy, and purpose of the various codes. The policies have long created a widely accepted relationship between dress restriction and effectiveness for a variety of situations: educational settings, societal roles, appropriateness, and professional success to name a few.

Briana Bell, history teacher

Sources of Information

Gathering reliable and useful information helps us more deeply understand the challenge that we identify through our collaborative work. We move forward discovering, examining, and synthesizing information from multiple sources that are known to us. We consider other possible sources as they are unearthed while we seek possible sources that may be unknown to us. What takes center stage in this book, as we discussed previously, is attaining knowledge—finding truths from the evidence that we collect in its diverse forms from data to social consensus, expert opinion, and knowledge available in literature. Evidence collected in the field so that we can better answer our research question(s) and pass our collective learning on to future generations through various print, visuals, audio, and digital forms.

In this chapter we examine not only our access to what is known but consider what is possible within the parameters of time, financial and human resources, and ethical considerations. We dedicate this chapter to presenting a systematic and logical way to review existing knowledge, which in turn may help engaged researchers to maximize the use of digital resources. We present steps to develop a plan to search databases for background information, utilize existing web-based applications to help us reference literature in an easy and effective manner, digitally document unwritten source material, analyze evidence, and synthesize what is known in order to build and write the literature review of a collaborative action research report. For both the researcher and the research project the review: (a) provides authority (as a person who knows), (b) strengthens one's voice, and (c) avoids reinventing what is already known by finding new and refreshing ways, angles to study a challenge.

Identifying Sources

Identifying the probable sources of information for the collaborative action research project and considering the team's access to that information determines the initial scope and potential for a meaningful study. The principal research team begins by brainstorming an exhaustive list of information that would benefit the study—student work samples, teacher interviews, district assessment data, observation data, past research, etc. (see Table 4.1).

Table 4.1: Sources of Information and Access

Information	Source	Access
Dress Code Policies	School/District	Yes
Research Articles	Library, Journals	Yes
Current Events	Newspapers	Yes
Observations	School	Maybe
Referrals	School Records	Yes
Interviews	Teachers	Yes
Interviews	Students	Maybe

Source: G. Arriaza and L. Scott © 2020

Next, the team notes how each item on their list would contribute to answering the research question broadly and ground-level questions specifically. Sources that would provide duplicative information are connected, and then those that would be crucial to the analysis highlighted. Finally, the team considers the access that they have to each unique source of information. Examples may include teachers' ability to provide student work samples, the feasibility of conducting interviews with students or their family member, access to libraries or databases, or administrative access to individual or aggregate student records. In each case, the team must determine the importance of each data point and whether it is required or desired.

For instance, the principal research team in this chapter's vignette began by brainstorming a list of items relevant to their work. They would need copies of the dress code policies for the districts and schools. They wondered about the history of dress code bias in schools, the consequences of dress bias, and how dress codes negatively affect each gender, especially how school learning environments are partially dependent on what female students wear. They asked the purpose of dress codes in schools and who the dress codes were written for and who decides what dress codes create an effective (or non-distracting) learning environment. They also brainstormed potential solutions. In each case they listed the possible information that would help them understand dress codes and considered their access to the sources of this information.

There is much information to consider, however once you are engaged in a topic that you have selected then you become the expert and are motivated to deepen your knowledge from a variety of sources found in different locations and formats. Searching libraries and online databases for archived documents in various formats—text, sound, visuals, film, and other digital formats—yields an understanding of what is already known about a topic and allows us to evaluate the evidence that underlies it. Empirical research reports, commonly published in academic journals, provide the original reports of the research. Information contained in these journal articles contributes to the understanding of researchers conducting future studies. They synthesize this information for their own reviews of the literature as the team in this chapter's vignette did in writing the literature review of their collaborative action research report. Magazine and newspaper articles, films, speeches, and arts serve as complementary material which corroborate and extend the evidence that we find. Sources, such as observations and interviews, also serve as data points which the team collects and analyzes. Any source of information that connects to the focal issue or problem has the potential to be among the sources of information identified by the team—unpublished manuscripts, oral histories, testimonials, student work, videos, photographs, murals, billboards, social media posts, signs, observations, interviews, policies, laws, standards, internet resources, and research-based programs or interventions.

Books related to the topic at hand are another source to understand what is already known about a topic. Books are often targeted to specific audiences. For instance, there may be books on school dress codes written for school administrators, teachers, or policy makers. Books may consider social as well as educational implications of policies. Authors who write books based on their research may frame their study or present implications of their work differently depending on the audience for the book.

A thesis or dissertation written on the topic at hand provides information that has been reviewed by other academics in the same field, similar to how academic journal articles are reviewed. Several organizations provide abstracts of these works which can be found in university archives. These works alert us to progress and discovery within the field we are studying. References cited in the manuscript may also guide us to further sources of information.

Oral histories are personal commentaries and information given by individuals, often older persons, to document events earlier in the individual's life that might otherwise be unrecorded. Researchers, historians, family members, or others record these memories, frequently through interviews, to preserve meaningful events so that they are not forgotten. Oral histories provide historical context for how the individual experienced history and fill in gaps in our historical knowledge. They also may help us understand the individual's experience or unique insight and may be the only source of information we have about an event or person.

The documentation and recorded interview of an individual's oral history (see Figure 4.1) follows a systematic plan with the formulation of questions related to a central issue, background information researched about the issue, interview recorded using a semi-structured format, the recording stored or archived, and the recording presented to the individual for further commentary.

Figure 4.1: Oral history documentation process
Source: G. Arriaza and L. Scott © 2020

Testimonios share similarities with oral histories, however they differ in that they may originate in written or oral formats and they emphasize that an individual is speaking for themselves in the first person "I" rather than having others speak or write on their behalf. Testimonios as first person narratives present autobiographical information in a unique, personal way that explains the individual's position to the information in a manner that adds credibility and persuades others of the information's importance. Testimonios give voice to individuals as they struggle against powerful forces that would silence their voices and erase their eyewitness accounts.

Sources such as student work, photographs, videos, and environmental information (e.g., signs, billboards, or landscapes) are also potential resources that provide us with data on our topic and can be documented in written, audio, or visual formats for analysis. Unpublished manuscripts are among the least authoritative sources of information. They may have been written initially as a research paper or as notes in personal collections or university archives and may be most helpful in guiding us to other published information or references and alerting us to lines of thinking within the field that lead us to additional sources of information.

Newspaper articles, whether published online or in print, are often current events or feature articles that provide insight into the topic, however they, as well as magazine articles, may contain opinions of the author that are not necessarily substantiated by scientific literature. For each of these article types it is important to confirm that the information is reported by multiple sources, determine if the information reported is opinion or news, and know the source of the information and credentials of the author.

Access to Sources

We access existing sources of information by investigating local archives, searching the internet, visiting the library, recording oral histories, collecting testimonios and student work, and photographing signs, billboards, and arts. For instance, the team researching the impact of student dress codes began by having each member search the university library's database for potential abstracts and then choosing articles to read. These included journal articles such as "Eliminating gender stereotypes in the public school dress codes; the necessity of respecting personal preferences" (Smith, 2012) published in the *Journal of Law in Education (JLE)* and newspaper articles such as "Littleton High Girls Call Schools' Dress Codes Sexist" (Hanson, 2015) published in *The Lowell Sun*. They also looked in their school archives for the dress code policy approved by their district school board.

The principal research team's access to experts, published information, and other knowledgeable sources varies depending on whether the individual is known to them or publications are publicly available. Once identified, experts and other knowledgeable individuals provide information through interviews, observations, surveys, and questionnaires as methods mentioned previously. Much information can be freely collected in public spaces or easily accessed online through free source or educational institutional access unless it is an individual's protected personal data or restricted for educational purposes. For instance, a collaborative action research team examining students' social interactions during the school day might freely collect information about the schedules of class activities at the school or demographics of a study body, however, they would be unlikely to have unrestricted access to students' attendance records, teachers' lesson plans, or school discipline records without seeking special permissions. Any brainstorm of the evidence that the team needs to consider and evaluate should include alternate sources if the specific data that the team deems as required is not available.

Credibility of Sources

To determine the level of credibility of a source of information, we consider the credentials of the individual, author, publication, or organization. For example, a journalist employed by *The Lowell Sun* wrote the newspaper article about the Littleton High students (Hanson, 2015). A search for information about the newspaper shows that at the time of the article's publication, it was a daily newspaper with separate news and opinion departments with a circulation of approximately 40,000 copies throughout its local region (www.lowellsun.com). While it is not possible to obtain information about the author's knowledge of the field, it is possible to read other news and feature articles by the author which are accessible in the newspaper's online archives. Further research about the newspaper's publisher(s), editor(s), and audience would provide substantiation of its credibility in the region. Additionally, several organizations provide web-based information about the factual accuracy of the mass media, politicians, and businesses. This may range from staff members researching statements, television ads, or news releases for false or misleading claims or serving to dispel discredited rumors or social media hoaxes.

For research publications, we consider the reputation of the editors and the process of review that the article underwent before it was accepted for publication. For example, Smith's (2012) article in the *JLE* was peer-reviewed by scholars in the field of educational law. Peer-review means not only that an expert in the field wrote the article on school dress codes but that several other experts scrutinized it before the journal publish it. Other experts' peer-review provides feedback to the editor to determine the article's suitability for acceptance for publication. Peer-review gives stronger assurance of the quality of the study and greater potential that its findings are scientifically valid and its conclusions reasonable.

A journal's reputation is also bolstered by its affiliation with the institutions responsible for its publication. For example, the *JLE* is published through the collaborative work of the respective law schools of the University of South Carolina and the University of Louisville. It is a resource for practitioners such as teachers, school administrators, judges, and lawyers who follow developments in education law nationally and internationally. In each *JLE* publication there is information about the composition of its editorial board and the institutional affiliation of its editors, reviewers, and university scholars in its publications and on its website (law.sc.edu/jled).

For every expert that provides research information we need to consider a few key areas: (a) legitimacy of credentials, (b) knowledge of the specific field being researched, (c) independence from the challenge so that to reduce bias and conflict of interest, (d) easy access to both the expert as well as to diverse data points.

The legitimacy of experts' credentials helps us determine their credibility and whether we can rely on the information they provide. As we articulate our ideas on a topic for our research team, having quality sources from experts strengthens our arguments. Credentials include academic degrees, diplomas, publications, institutional affiliation, association memberships, professional responsibilities, etc. If the expert has published books, written articles, or given speeches, we can consider others' reviews of their works. We also can evaluate the evidence that they use to support claims in their works. Information that they use to support the ideas in their works shows the depth of their knowledge of the field. Experts build their arguments by referencing other works and showing how their ideas extend our knowledge or fill in gaps in our understanding.

Experts display their independence when they can freely share their ideas and evidence without limitations and conflicts of interest. Information provided by experts who adhere to institutional and governmental requirements to minimize bias and conflicts of interest disclose their roles and responsibilities and identify existing and potential relationships which may impact the quality of information that they report.

Diversity of Source Authors

As discussed previously, in order to successfully plan and conduct a research project, four core elements ought to be present: a supportive and functional organizational practice; leadership capacity at all levels; a robust, diverse, and available set of evidentiary materials; and the availability of technologies to implement an appropriate collaborative action research. Functional organizational practice and leadership capacity pertain to culture; data sets and technology belong to structures. Pulsing through each these core elements is not only what has been written on this topic but especially who has written on it.

Data show the importance of diversity in our organizations, which fosters increased productivity, greater creativity, and innovation (Sousa & Clark, 2018). Diversity leads to people becoming more engaged and through collaborative action research sharing and respecting other voices. Perrin (2018) informs us to seek diversity through: (a) multiple approaches to studying the topic at hand, (b) diverse sources representing various publishers and publication formats, (c) a variety of publication dates through the years, and (d) diverse voices that are not traditionally heard, such as those of women, immigrants, refugees, people of color, LGBTQ, and youth.

Providing a space for diverse voices is not only an ethical concern but a pragmatic concern for our well-being. We need awareness of how to address issues of mental health in our local and academic communities. For instance within academic research, Sousa and Clark (2018) note that up to half of early career researchers and students face challenges to their mental health with even greater incidences for those involved in qualitative research. Outlets for published research privilege certain perspectives over others and erect barriers to maintain its privilege. For instance, the peer-review process discussed previously shapes what individuals and groups are represented in spaces where knowledge is shared. This process determines what is possible for discussion and debate, creating boundaries of what is normal or legitimate for discussion. While social media has democratized the sharing of diverse perspectives—anyone can post their thoughts—in academic journals, there is a process to becoming prominent and developing the skills to become influential, which can leave alternative voices on the periphery. Thus, it is important that our team seeks the perspectives of diverse, emerging researchers in new formats such as webinars, teacher communities, practitioner research, etc. so that we gain a more complete picture of our world and ensure that voices from around the world are included in our work without constraints based on socioeconomic status, geographic location, or mobility.

A good starting point to find evidence is in the literature. As this published evidence is known to us it provides our team with a basic understanding of our topic. We evaluate the strength of evidence and seek new evidence that was unknown—or unknown to us—to further what we know. We consider the credibility of the evidence, and as we discussed in Chapter Three, it is critical for question design to have validity and reliability so that surveys, interviews, and questionnaires yield meaningful data. While conflicting evidence may provide for fruitful collaborative discussions, inaccurate data or false information can undermine any potential benefits of a study. Through our collective work, we seek to make connections among items of credible evidence in order to enlarge and deepen our growing understanding of the topic at hand. In the following section, we consider accessing evidence found in specific sources of information and establishing a process for synthesizing the various works cited in the literature review.

The Literature Review

The literature review should emphasize first-hand, primary sources of information. It is important to read the original research ourselves to clear up any doubts we may have about a secondary sources' review, summary, or conclusion. Literature is considered *primary source information* when the author(s) share their findings or ideas from their original study or theoretical literature. It is the first published report and commonly includes the methodology, findings, and implications of the research. Reading a published primary source shows us if there were any limitations to the original research study, and it explains the study's methodology and why researchers set up their study the way they did.

For example, the team in this chapter's vignette read a published study (about dress code enforcement in an ethnically diverse high school), discussed its main ideas, and drew their own conclusions as a team. They noted the methods used by the article authors: interviewing 13 randomly selected teachers and surveying all of the school's 1,200 students with 384 students responding. They selected a key quote for discussion: "The survey found that Black and multiracial students were disproportionately likely to be 'coded' (spoken to by a school adult) or disciplined for dress code violations" (Pavlakis & Roegman, 2018, p. 1). And, they synthesized information and drew their own conclusions of what ideas were important to include in their literature review, such as dress code policies that seem neutral with regards to gender but affect females, and students of color, differently.

Secondary sources of information are reports of the ideas and research of others. Wikipedia, encyclopedias, textbooks, research summaries, and books that give an overview of what others have written are secondary sources. This also includes television, newspaper, and mass media reports that give a broad overview of a topic or report second-hand information. They do not report original data but rather summarize others' data and present the conclusions of the original authors. In referencing secondary sources of information we are accepting the opinion of others rather than judging the research for ourselves (Krathwohl, 2009; Perrin, 2018).

Secondary sources are not first-hand accounts, and they usually do not provide the methods used to obtain the information. For instance, the thesis *A Review of the Current Literature, Both Pro and Con, Concerning the Use of School Uniforms* (Ajayi, 2010) provides us with the author's summary of information from 1950 to 2010 about school uniforms, important court cases about school dress codes, and the implementation of related policies. The analysis of controversies is from the author's perspective, and the selection of pro and con arguments presented come from the author's judgment. The conclusion drawn—that the literature does not provide evidence of school uniform policies and student behavior being correlated—also belongs to the author. Reading secondary sources is helpful in giving us a general idea of the breadth of the research and others' analysis. References listed in secondary sources of information also often direct us to seminal works and publications containing primary source information.

Peer-Reviewed, Published Research

We seek legitimate sources of information such as peer-reviewed books and research articles published in academic journals to synthesize and cite in the literature review. Authors with specialized knowledge in the field publish peer-reviewed empirical research in print or online academic journals. These sources hold the highest authority among published information. They report primary source information, which builds upon the existing knowledge in the field and also follows a particular format and process (see Figure 4.2).

Figure 4.2: Research article format example
Source: G. Arriaza and L. Scott © 2020

Authors of research articles begin by introducing the topic and reviewing pertinent literature on the topic at hand, next describing the methods that they used to collect and analyze the data in their study, then presenting the findings from their research, and finally discussing the implications of these findings and suggesting areas for further research. The kinds of studies presented in research articles vary from experiments and surveys to interviews and observation; however, all studies present raw data that the authors collected and analyzed along with the conclusions that the authors drew from the findings of that analysis. Authors always reference other works in their research article and use these references to situate their research and bolster the discussion of their findings.

Within each published research article authors describe their methods used, which may include interviews, observations, questionnaires, and surveys (see also Chapter Five). For instance, authors describe interviews of individuals as semi-structured, structured, or unstructured interviews. Semi-structured interviews are those in which the research team developed a list of questions that they used in the interview and then posed follow-up questions during the interview based on the interviewee's responses. Structured interviews resemble a verbally presented questionnaire with a specific, pre-determined set of questions that were thoroughly tested in a lengthy process to elicit maximum information. Structured interview questions are not altered during the interview. On the other hand, unstructured interviews, with few or no formal interview questions, are conversational in style focusing the interview on the topic at hand; thus, authors may report them as anecdotal information.

In the article's method section, researchers also report data from observations of individuals or groups. Common forms of observation include naturalistic observation, structured observation, and participant-observation. If researchers used structured observations in the study, they explain how they controlled the observation by artificially creating situations in order to observe the specific behaviors that they are interested in. Through naturalistic observation occurring in the field or natural environment, researchers report the behaviors of individuals or groups that they viewed, and they explain how they systematically recorded specific features, utterances, or interactions. Another method of observation is participant-observation, which is similar to naturalistic observation with the variation that the researchers are among those being observed. In this case, they are embedded in order to obtain a deeper understanding of the group.

Additionally, collecting data through questionnaires and surveys is another method that researchers use. A questionnaire is a written list of questions asked of an individual, which is made up of many questions to compile details such as personal opinions or demographic data in order to provide a broader picture of the participants. Among the question types are yes-no, true-false, open-ended, multiple choice, or short answer. Surveys are like questionnaires in that they both have a list of questions, but a survey takes into account the methods used in collecting the data and analyzing the responses. When reading articles reporting studies with these methods, it is important to note the number of participants and whether these participants are a representative sample of individuals with demographics that mirror a larger group targeted by the researchers.

Authors of these articles build on the published work of others by extending, refining, or re-examining ideas and findings. They offer us ways to think about our problem within the context of previously published research. By comparing and contrasting our ideas with the published work of others, we are able to better conceptualize our problem and articulate it in a way that is more feasible to study. Understanding the published work on our topic also provides us with a deeper understanding of the variables—and the relationships among the variables—in our research question(s) that we discussed in Chapter Three. Learning what is known about our problem by linking it to published research improves our ability to go beyond existing research without rediscovering what is already known. It potentially helps us avoid the mistakes of other researchers resulting in more effective use of our time, less expense, and improved methods in conducting our study (Krathwohl, 2009).

Peer-reviewed research comes in the form of empirical and theoretical studies. Empirical studies are research conducted within the physical world or a social organizations such as a school. Empirical means observation, and empirical research means systematic observation. As we read the research literature it is important to note whether the researchers' methods included systematic observation—planned with care to justify who the researchers observed, how they conducted the observation, and what features they observed.

Building and adding to our empirical knowledge is an iterative process that is continually changing and growing. Empirical research does not offer proof, but rather it provides degrees of evidence. Stronger degrees of evidence are considered more influential in understanding the problem addressed in the research than studies with lower degrees of evidence. For instance, study limitations impact our ability to infer any findings on a broader group when there is a small n (number of observed participants). How researchers identify the problem limits what we can infer because research studies only looking at a small piece of the problem might be overlooking many other aspects that could impact the larger problem. Multiple measures offer stronger degrees of evidence as they are better than one measure in case one measure is flawed. Thus, any points of knowledge described as facts are actually not; they just help us have more confidence in the findings.

The purpose of a theoretical study is to offer new theories, perspectives, or positions on a topic based on existing research or prior theoretical proposals. A theoretical study can also be a meta-analysis of existing research that brings together a set of studies to corroborate patterns and overarching truths in the empirical research.

Consulting and using the empirical and theoretical research as evidence makes up the body of work captured in the literature review section of a research project, however, published reports of oral histories, testimonios, and anecdotal reports can be valuable in the literature review to corroborate the published peer-reviewed empirical research that we review. An anecdote describes something that happened or made an impression. It is not based on systematic observation, and thus offers evidence but not necessarily the stronger evidence that we seek in which to situate our problem. It may be a personal experience or something of teaching practice or technique that someone is reporting about. Anecdotal information cannot be used exclusively, and it needs to be noted that it is anecdotal.

Additional primary sources of information considered as published—but not necessarily peer-reviewed—information include maps, lectures, speeches, radio programs, photographs, motion pictures, television shows, paintings, signs, student work, and information in our physical environment such as murals, landscapes, and community information. They appear in audio, video, or other electronic formats, and in some cases, such as lectures or radio/television content, are secondary or primary sources of information. (Perrin, 2018). Whenever we reference such information we should note whether it has undergone peer-review or other scientific examination.

Developing a System to Manage What Is Known

A systematic way of finding out everything we know is like set of concentric circles. The immediate group of individuals is the inner circle, and you are the dot in the middle. As discussed previously we brainstorm, we interview experts, we systematically observe. Now, we search databases to find original research and theoretical literature, and we develop a system to keep track of what we know and are learning. In order to keep track of everything that we know we develop a system built around the concentric circles.

Table 4.2: Research Table of Study Type, Description, and Key Findings

Reference	Type of Study	Description of Study	Key Findings
Pavlakis, A., & Roegman, R. (2018). How dress codes criminalize males and sexualize females of color. *Phi Delta Kappan, 100*(2), 54–58.	Survey	School dress codes and their enforcement impact students differently based on gender and race at high school in the Midwest.	Surveyed students perceived school dress codes as unfair. Black and multiracial students disproportionately disciplined or verbally warned for dress code violations. Girls' dress code violations called distracting and overly revealing. Black males dress code violations perceived as associated with criminality.

Source: G. Arriaza and L. Scott © 2020

Building Tables to Summarize the Literature

For the literature review, we take a comprehensive look at primary source documents and build tables to summarize the literature. We create a literature matrix, map, or web that connects to the team's list of information. We want to your work to be up-to-date and thorough, so our table (see Table 4.2) needs to show the time of publication range and reference, in addition to specific information about the study such as its type, description, purpose, or relationship to our own study.

Building a table of research methods (see Table 4.3) used in the published works cited provides valuable information that organizes key information. The principal research team must decide what to include in the table. For example, the methods report participant recruitment, sample size, and describe participant characteristics.

Table 4.3: Research Methods Table

Reference	Participant Recruitment	Sample Size	Participant Characteristics
Pavlakis, A., & Roegman, R. (2018). How dress codes criminalize males and sexualize females of color. *Phi Delta Kappan, 100*(2), 54–58.	Invited all students at one high school in the Midwest; Random sample of teachers	n = 1,200 students invited; n = 384 students responded n = 13 teachers interviewed	about 40% White, 35% Black, 10% Latino, and 10% multiracial; about two-thirds of the students are classified as economically disadvantaged.

Source: G. Arriaza and L. Scott © 2020

Keeping a Table of Definitions

Tracking how different authors in your literature review define items, variables, or terms enables the team to readily compare terminology. This table may be different from or similar to your principle research team's list of definitions (see Chapter Three). By placing both lists alongside each other the team is able to review both lists of definitions to see the differences and similarities in definitions or to see if the same concept has multiple definitions.

Managing Time

Figuring out the amount of time that you have and scheduling specific blocks of time in your calendar in order to prepare your literature review prepares you to manage the demands of the team's schedule and meet shared deadlines (see Table 4.4). Team members propose and agree on a topic, read and share an analysis of articles, organize notes into a synthesis of new thinking, and find new data points. Throughout, they provide feedback and review of each aspect at agreed upon times that move the project forward. Estimating the time needed to gather the data also impact the research work. In some cases investing time in gaining authorization to use one, otherwise restricted, source might be more efficient than the group collecting multiple sources of publicly available, comparable information.

Table 4.4: Literature Review Schedule

	1st Draft	Review 1	Review 2	Final Version
Select Topic	Sept. 30	Oct. 15	Oct. 20	Oct. 30
Read and Analyze Articles	Oct 30	Nov. 15	Dec. 1	Dec. 30
Organize Synthesize	Jan. 30	Feb. 15	Feb. 28	March 15
Find New Data Points	Feb. 28	March 15	March 30	April 30

Source: G. Arriaza and L. Scott © 2020

It is not possible to review endless resources, so it is important to break the process of writing the literature review into a series of small steps in a multistep process beginning with your search of available literature.

Search Basics

Gone are the days of roaming the library in search of sources—it is more hit and miss due to changing physical resources, availability, and missing books. Searching online databases is a better place to start. Librarians can orient you to the resources, and online tutorials provide guidance.

Begin with the general topic that your team selects to see how much literature you can find on the topic. Depending on the amount of literature that your search yields, reduce the number of items so that your search on the topic is more manageable. The search could be only journal articles, or since a certain date, or with certain key words. The literature that you identify related to the general topic informs your research team as you finalize your topic.

When your team agrees to the selected topic, determine the key ideas to be addressed in the literature review and search for a limited number of publications on each idea. Start with a search limited to the most recent five years, then expand the search depending on the number of publications retrieved. Reviewing the works cited frequently in the most recent publications points you to seminal publications from prior years. Finally, you review only these seminal publications from the prior decade.

Becoming Familiar with Online Databases

Several search possibilities exist for finding scholarly literature related to your topic. Avoid starting your search using a general internet search engine as the quality of the data you receive, and the credibility of the source is unknown. An exception is Google Scholar (scholar.google.com) which broadly searches for scientific articles, academic books, open-access journals, conference proceedings, and other scholarly information by scanning education domain (.edu) and other webpages. Its search tools allow you to locate articles by title and to restrict the date range of publications and types of information. Additionally, under each item it identifies in your search, a *Cited by* tab allows you to expand your search to search any literature referencing the original item. Google Scholar does not, however, consider the reputation or credibility of the sources that publish the information, so it is helpful only if used in conjunction with specialized databases for education.

Your university librarians are essential partners in supporting your search for scholarly literature found in specialized databases for education. They help you find out what databases are used in your field of study and which are available at your institution's library. They also explain the library databases that you have access to and their organization as well as the software of the vendors that your institution has agreements with.

For example, ERIC, ProQuest, EBSCOhost, PsycINFO, and Educator's Reference Complete each have databases with links to abstracts or scholarly literature found in practitioner publications and academic books. By logging in through your institution's library and using a specialized database you find the full-text of articles that you have access to. This helps you save time by avoiding items found by general search engine but unavailable to you.

ERIC (eric.ed.gov) is the Educational Resources Information Center—commonly known by its acronym—and is a database sponsored by the Institute of Education Sciences of the U.S. Department of Education. It is freely available and accessed online. The users of its database include educational researchers, academics, policy makers, educators, post-secondary students, and the general public. Scholarly literature included in the ERIC database comes from comprehensively and selectively indexed journals. ERIC follows a selection criteria to comprehensively index journals that have over 80% education-related articles. It also selectively indexes education-related articles from other journals that are critical to education. In its collection ERIC maintains a bibliographic record of articles published in a variety of approved journal sources as well as educational information funded or produced by governmental entities, such as the U.S. Department of Education, federal technical assistance providers, state and local agencies, and programs affiliated with universities. It also indexes non-governmental educational information from educational non-profits, policy organizations, professional associations, publishers, and international education organizations.

ProQuest is a library database vendor that provides access to curated academic materials and content accessed online only after signing into a university library or other gateway. It allows you to cross-search research topics across multiple formats and immediately access the full-text of many articles indexed in ERIC. ProQuest includes scholarly journals, dissertations, and theses of graduate students, working papers, eBooks, newspapers, periodicals, governmental and cultural archives, and historical collections from museums and prominent organizations. Since being founded in Michigan as University Microfilms in 1938, it has expanded into electronic publishing and structuring researchers' search for data. Today we no longer need to spend hours sorting through microfilm and microfiche in the physical library.

The EBSCO*host* is similar to ProQuest in that you must access it through your university library or other gateway. It is useful because the full-text of many documents indexed by ERIC is available immediately through the databases it searches. EBSCO*host* allows you to search databases including general reference collections as well as subject-specific educational databases such as APA PsycInfo from the American Psychological Association.

The APA PsycInfo library database has education and psychology books, book chapters, summaries of journal articles, and dissertations dating back to 1840, all accessed through your institution's library. APA PsycNet (psycnet.apa.org) contains abstracts and some full-text articles of peer-reviewed educational research literature. Educator's Reference Complete is a database that contains research literature and is used by college librarians as well as public schools and teachers for online learning in the classroom. Librarians also advise scholars to search databases from other fields concerned with children, adolescents, mental health, society, sociology, social services, and economics literature for information on school finance.

In addition to the APA, the webpages of other national organizations such as the American Educational Research Association (aera.net/Publications) and the National Association for Multicultural Education (nameorg.org/mcp_journal.php) serve as centers of knowledge and have peer-reviewed, educational literature online.

Using Descriptors

Each library database has a set of descriptors that aid in your search. Descriptors are index terms that librarians or similar individuals assign to articles. Using the descriptors helps us be laser focused and precise in our search. For example, using the descriptor *dress codes* for any article about *school policies regarding permitted student clothing* would retrieve similar articles. Using non-descriptors like *attire* or *code* would not retrieve related articles or might retrieve unrelated articles. PsycInfo has a complete list of its descriptors in the link *APA Thesaurus of Psychological Index Terms* at the top of its library database webpage. ERIC and Educator's Reference Complete each have the link *Thesaurus* which directs you to a full list of their descriptors. Each ERIC bibliographic record contains the assigned descriptors for the record.

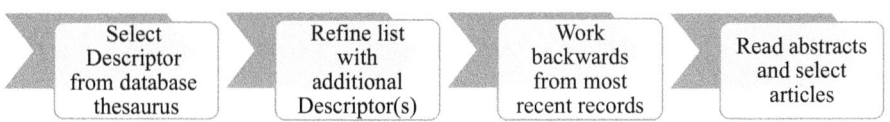

Figure 4.3: Formulating a search with descriptors
Source: G. Arriaza and L. Scott © 2020

To formulate a search of the database, put a descriptor in the search bar and determine the size of the list retrieved (see Figure 4.3). Next, refine the size of the list by adding additional descriptors. In some databases you separate the descriptors with *AND* to narrow the search; *OR* to broaden the search. Then, work backwards from the most recently published research. Finally, read the abstracts that are brief summaries of the article to give you an idea of the article and help you decide which to read the full text.

For example, an ERIC search using the descriptor *Dress Codes* retrieves a few hundred records. The descriptor *Freedom of Speech* retrieves a few thousand records! Narrowing the search by using both descriptors retrieves under a hundred records common to both. Working backwards there are about 10 abstracts in the past decade and about 20 abstracts in the past score. Reading the abstracts that are brief summaries of the article gives an idea. Reviewing this initial group of literature resources stimulates us to ask which articles might make a useful contribution (Creswell, 2009). The following abstract from the article *Say What? The Principal's T-Shirt Conundrum* was among the recent records.

> In today's public secondary schools, administrators face challenges that prior generations never anticipated, one of which is the T-shirt conundrum. The T-shirts that students wear to class contain all sorts of messages and images, many of which administrators may well consider inappropriate. This article is intended to help beleaguered educators sort out which messages and images are protected by law and which may be censored by administrative disciplinary action. Recent controversies are examined through an overview of federal court rulings. The article then concludes with some practical guidelines for educators and school boards. (McDaniel, 2016, p. 13)

The information in the abstract relates closely to the school dress code topic discussed in this chapter's vignette, so adding it to a list of 50 published works to consider for our literature review is appropriate. In order to thematically organize possible literature by important concepts we need to establish priorities for the literature selection. The abstract considers the perspective of the secondary school administrator which could be a theme—protected freedom of speech, court rulings, and school policies yet other themes.

It is useful to consider the descriptors associated with each article to guide you to other information. This chapter's descriptors from the ERIC thesaurus were guidelines, dress codes, school policy, and freedom of speech. Returning to search the ERIC records by combining the descriptors *dress codes* and *school policy* is a potential further step. In some cases adding the descriptors *action research, meta-study/meta, theory,* or *review* to *dress code* to a further search would retrieve theoretical articles or review articles connected to the topic.

Note: Do not confuse *descriptors* with *key words*. Article authors often select key words to accompany the title and abstract of their article.

Maintaining a List of References

A reference list is a list of every published work that is cited in the literature review. Usually the reference list appears at the end of written work though it can also appear at the end of each chapter or as an endnote or footnote. An especially important example of a reference is a *seminal* work in the field. We consider a published work seminal if it significantly impacted the field. Seminal works are often those that other authors cite frequently across their published literature on a topic. A citation, or in-text citation, occurs in the written text to indicate that the idea or quote comes from another author. We write in-text citations in a shortened form according to APA style (Perrin, 2018) to correspond to the full reference:

Perrin, R. (2018). *Pocket guide to APA style* (6th Ed.). Stamford, CT: Cengage.

which appears on the list of references.

The principal research team maintains a working reference list throughout the development of the literature review. When the team cites a reference in the final literature review, they highlight the reference on the working list to assure that only references cited in the final literature review appear on the final list of references.

Several free online reference tools, such as Zotero.com (see resources), immediately populate in your document after you cite a work from your list of references in the literature review.

Reading and Analyzing Published Information

Through our search and reading the abstracts, we find many records of published works to include in our literature review. It is important that we read closely any work that we cite in the literature review so that we understand the details and the author's methods, findings, and arguments. Reading only reviews, summaries, or abstracts of articles has the potential to give a false sense of what the article is about.

Now it is time to read each work, and think about what you have read. For a research article, (see Figure 4.4) first read a few paragraphs for an overview of the problem that the author is laying out. Next, scan the text, reading the headings and subheadings throughout, to get an idea of how the author organized the article. Tompkins (2017) gives a good perspective on the need to start any reading activity with pre-reading so that you notice the features of the text that signal key ideas and contributions by the author to record in your notes. This specific pre-reading activity is not meant as a word-for-word reading of the text but rather to give yourself an overview of the entire work that you are about to read.

Figure 4.4: Reading a research article
Source: G. Arriaza and L. Scott © 2020

Then, go back and read the paragraphs just before the Methods section. You should find the research question(s) in these paragraphs. Normally just after the author of the text lays out the literature review, they end the section by pointing out gaps in the literature and state the research questions. They may also point to theoretical aspects that merit a deeper dive. Once authors state the research questions, they describe the methods that they used to examine the topic. Finally, read the literature review carefully to identify the major theories that the author discusses and make a note if they connect closely to your topic. Continue reading the article examining the methods described, findings, implications of the findings, and calls for future research.

Notetaking and Annotations
In order to analyze the information that we selected to closely read we need to be systematic in our notes and annotations because we have many sources. A principal research team that identifies approximately 50 published works to read must be organized in its note-taking so that the final literature review is complete and reflects the available knowledge. The team must maintain a reference list using APA style (Perrin, 2018), and if they quote any passages, they must include the page numbers in their notes and citation in the final literature review.

Verifying the quotes and page numbers is an easy step to brush off, but re-reading the quote word-for-word and double-checking the page number now avoids the need to go back to the text and hunt for the quote later. Following the same step of verifying any statistics in the research written in the notes assures that the team accurately introduces the information and problem to readers of the final literature review. Using precise statistics (e.g., 65% of students saw clothing choice as free speech) is more descriptive than writing over half, thus precision in note-taking from the outset is critical.

When reading the research study described in the literature, note if it is qualitative or quantitative. Each research study type (see Table 4.5) has different features such as how researchers state the hypothesis, select its participant sample, collect data, analyze data, and report findings. Record in your notes the study type and salient features of the research study.

Table 4.5: Features of Research Studies and Methods

Quantitative Study	Hypothesis is explicitly stated, guides the study;
	Sample is unbiased, without selection bias, often random, representative of larger population, significant due to large size 1,000+ national participants or 25+ local participants for a trial;
	Data collected include surveys, questionnaires, tests
	Systematic observation described in detail;
	Findings are reported in statistics, can be inferred to larger group;
	Systematic analysis of evidence can prove hypothesis.
Qualitative Study	Methods include semi-structured interviews, observation;
	Sample small, participants purposefully selected; case study of 1+
	Data collected include interview quotes, observation field notes;
	Analysis examines data closely, over time
	Findings reported without statistics, quotes/notes explain patterns in data.
Qualitative Research	Mixed methods quantify qualitative data in numbers;
	Findings are patterns in the data, determined by the consensus of the research team after independent, individual analysis;
	Study participants check team's findings, give comments, share emic perspectives.
Longitudinal Study	Research is conducted over time;
	Researchers compare different time points.
Experimental Study	Quantitative study—normally;
	Some participants receive a treatment or change in condition;
	Control/comparison and intervention groups randomly assigned;
	Researchers measure change in participant condition.
Non-experimental Study	Qualitative or quantitative study;
	Participants do not receive a treatment or change in condition;
Quasi-experimental Study	Participants are not randomly assigned;
	Researchers manipulate independent variable (i.e., pretest-post-text, time change, nonequivalent groups design).

Continued

Table 4.5: *Continued*

Note: About Sample	Researchers purposefully select sample to provide rich study data, select a sample which is representative of the greater population, can infer findings of small sample on the greater population, describe participant characteristics; randomly assign participants to condition.

Source: G. Arriaza and L. Scott © 2020

Your notes should include the value of the information in each text that you review. This includes the relevance of the study and its findings, its similarity to other published works, and the credibility of the author(s) (Hendricks, 2013). Recording the authority of the authorship allows the research team to determine if an educational researcher with an advanced degree and scholarly training in the field authored the work and whether the author has current research and other publications in the field. These and the author' degree and academic affiliations establish their authority (Perrin, 2018). To establish the reputation of the publication, Perrin writes "University, academic, or trade presses publish most of the books you will use, which generally ensures their credibility" (p. 11).

An annotated bibliography is a good place to capture information from original research. Consult your detailed notes to write it concisely and critically. Its purpose is to note the published work's accuracy, relevance, and quality and the source's credibility and authority. Unlike abstracts—which are summaries located in an index or at the beginning of a journal article—an annotation concisely describes the research and critically notes the viewpoint of the work's author(s). An annotated bibliography includes whether ideas come from empirical research or the author's assertion (i.e., opinion). It also compares works on the list of references to guide the writing of the literature review (see Table 4.6).

Table 4.6: Parts of an Annotated Bibliography

Reference	McDaniel, T. (2016). Say What? The Principal's T-Shirt Conundrum. *American Secondary Education, 44*(3), 13–18.
Concise Description of the Research	Federal court rulings regarding freedom of speech and school dress code policies cause school administrators to carefully examine the situations when they can censure messages on student clothing. The author offers practical guidelines and guidance to navigating recent controversies.
Evaluate Author Authority and Point of View	The author is a professor emeritus who holds a Ph.D. and teaches school law. The journal audience is academics, teachers, and administrators who seek peer-reviewed information reporting teaching, teacher education, and administrative procedures in middle and high schools. School dress code policies must be clear, viewpoint neutral, and protect student learning.

Source: G. Arriaza and L. Scott © 2020

When the team has read the research information, detailed the key aspects of the research studies in notes and annotations, it is time to move toward the writing goal and bring together the annotated knowledge as a coherent narrative.

Writing the Literature Review

Your literature review is where you summarize, synthesize, and interpret research on your topic from your reading of the published works that you selected. Writing the literature review entails synthesizing the important themes that your team identified while reading, notetaking, and annotating the texts. You convey your message to your readers in a coherent logical form so that they follow your line of reasoning or argument.

It is important for the team to follow a deliberate process of writing in order to successfully complete the literature review in a reasonable timeframe (see Figure 4.5). The first step is planning and organizing the information, followed by writing a rough draft of the information, revising the draft, editing the grammar and mechanics, and finally publishing the literature review for your readers.

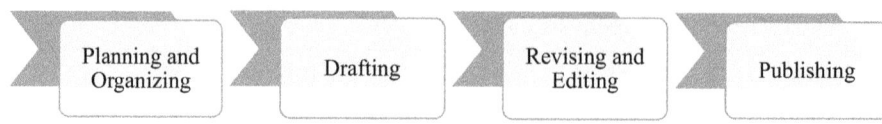

Figure 4.5: Writing process of a literature review
Source: G. Arriaza and L. Scott © 2020

Begin by organizing the information in your notes and annotations that you gathered as a result of the planning that you accomplished through agreeing on a topic and selecting relevant literature. Organizing your notes and annotated information helps you develop a detailed writing outline. Organizing also means analyzing, synthesizing, and evaluating the research literature that you reviewed. Your objective is to bring together the annotated knowledge as a coherent narrative, not to summarize cited works individually. Your readers want to understand your analysis of the information and your important themes, so it is important to synthesize the literature before writing.

By connecting, or mapping, the contributions of the literature that you review to the variables in your team's study (see Table 4.7), you set the stage for your readers to understand the need for your research team's study. The literature review that you write is an expository essay. That means that you describe and explain the existing research in a manner that supports your argument. Your problem statement that your team wrote regarding the topic to guide your research efforts is the initial guidepost. Then, lay out all of the notes that you have in an organized framework. This becomes your writing outline.

Table 4.7: Mapping the Literature to the Study

My Study's Variables	Match of Article/Book One List of Contributions to My Study's Variables	Match of Article/Book Two "P" Contributions to My Study's Variables
Variable X		
Variable Y		
Variable Z		

Source: G. Arriaza and L. Scott © 2020

As you begin drafting the literature review, consider your purpose and voice. Your perspective or angle about the general themes and specific issues you raise are of interest to your readers and present a compelling argument as to how this review illuminates your team's study. Near the beginning of the literature review, indicate to your readers what you will address in the review. Also explain what you will not address.

When possible move from general ideas to specific ideas stating the large central themes from your review and then linking them with specific ideas to your proposed study's purpose is an effective way to move from general to the specific. State a very clear thesis statement early in your review and then explain how your team's thesis relates to the problem and the independent and dependent variables that your research study examines. Your statement is a declarative statement that indicates to your readers that this is the specific topic that you will present in the review (Perrin, 2018). Also be sure to indicate that later in the review you will explain your evidence and point of view.

A deductive argument starts by stating a broad idea and then supporting it with details and information to substantiate it. However your team may choose to follow an inductive argument. An inductive argument starts from specific points and then builds with substantiating points to a broader more general idea. As you proceed with your review consider if you should follow a deductive or inductive argument in a later draft of your literature review. Regardless of your team's choice, you should structure the body of the review by bringing in all of the most salient research authors that you annotated and cite their seminal works when appropriate.

Explicitly explain why some studies are more important than others. If a work is seminal in the field, explain why it is groundbreaking and provide a summary of the key findings that connect to your team's study. If your study is a new area for research that directly stems from the seminal work, write that expressly. Also refer to any theoretical work that impacts your topic and whether this connects to any seminal works. Discuss how different studies in your literature review relate to theory or build theory.

Most importantly, explain to your readers why the topic your team chose is important. While it may not be important to everyone, its importance should be apparent to some. Explain the need for the research that you propose and whether it fills a gap in the research literature or that it includes the voices of sources that previous researchers have not included. If your team's purpose is to replicate a study in a new setting, your setting, then explain that as well.

Start each paragraph with a topic sentence. For example: Recognizing common activities and means of communication used in schools appears as a key first step to establish solid relationships with parents. Or, similar to the research team in this chapter's vignette: Recognizing how students' dress in high school and the messages that their clothing choices express requires thoughtful consideration in the development of school dress codes policies. If your topic sentence is an important quote from a reference, state the quote, paraphrase the quote in your own words, and give an example of the quote.

While quotes are effective evidence, your review should be a concise synthesis of the themes you noted in your reading of the scholarly literature on the topic at hand. Thus, your review should not be a series of direct quotations. Paraphrasing an idea synthesizes the idea more succinctly in your voice for your readers. An in-text citation after the synthesis directs your readers to the full reference where they have supporting information and details at hand.

Synthesizing is looking for patterns in your notes of the original research and reporting these patterns as themes in your review. If your review includes any meta-studies on the topic, report the empirical results and identify the scholarly works. Mentioning other reviews indicates to readers that you identified other works worthy of consideration even though you did not refer to the study in detail.

Review your notes to see how authors in your reference list substantiated any controversial evidence. It is always best to use uncontroversial evidence to substantiate each claim made in the literature review. It is important that your readers agree that the problem exists and not be dissuaded from your intentions because of controversial or unsubstantiated assertions. Triangulating the information that you present increases its credibility (see Chapter Five) and further substantiates your ideas. Triangulation is presenting multiple forms of evidence to ensure that fundamental ideas do not rely on a single form of evidence.

Final considerations for your first draft of the literature review are to report the time frame of studies that you report. Also explain any gaps in the literature and verify that you did not miss a topic because of the way that you conducted the search for scholarly literature. Throughout your review, you can incorporate tables into the text so that you present information in graphic organizers. You refer to any tables in your text and explain the important information.

At the end of each part of your literature review connect the key themes back to your thesis statement. Summarize what you wrote throughout to keep your readers abreast of the argument that you are laying out. It is a good idea to summarize the first three ideas before presenting the fourth and fifth ideas. Reiterating the key inferences, conclusions, main points, and themes keeps the reader engaged without having to skip back in the text.

At the very end of the literature review conclude by restating your thesis statement, offering concrete suggestions for future research, and restating the ideas that point to the research questions that arise from your team's literature review.

Revising the Literature Review

The next step in the process of writing the literature review is revising. This means rewriting what you wrote after carefully re-reading the themes that you presented and assuring that you substantiated each idea. Improving the layout of your literature review by organizing the text to better unfold and unpack your argument is also essential at this step.

Add transitional sentences to aid the readers understanding and serve a sign post for new information or ideas. Remove any annotations that appear in your first draft. While annotations were helpful in your organization and synthesis of the research information, they are not used in the literature review.

After you have revised your draft on one or more occasions, you now move to the next-to-the-last step in the writing process. In this step, you carefully attend to the mechanics of the literature review: the grammar, punctuation, mechanics, APA Style, accuracy, and flow (see Table 4.8). The final task of this editing step is to double-check that the team members used the words from your definition table consistently throughout the literature review. You use the same term consistently throughout the literature review rather than providing a word with a similar meaning, or synonym, for variety. The literature review requires the use of precise, concise, consistent, and conventional terminologies.

Table 4.8: Mechanics of the Literature Review

Review the topic sentences in each paragraph.
Change any instances of passive voice to active voice.
Check the details cited.
Cite all information and ideas that appears in your reviewed work.
Include the page number in the in-text citation of any quoted passage.
Confirm that your in-text citations are in the latest APA edition (Perrin, 2018).
Follow the style manual for correct references.
Use a formal narrative without abbreviations.
Use etc. (and so forth), e.g. (for example), i.e. (that is), vs. (versus), et al. (and others).
Confirm that each acronym is spelled out the first time it appears.
Double-check the consistency of the words used from the definition table.

Source: G. Arriaza and L. Scott © 2020

In conclusion, after following these steps it is finally time to share our literature review and pose our research questions. We do this because we searched, gathered, analyzed, and synthesized scholarly research information to help us understand our research problem. We have substantiated key themes from multiple sources in what is known to guide us in our collaborative work. We now move forward to select the methods to use in order to collect data, analyze data, and find new understanding from our collaborative work. As we do, we continue to consider other possible sources as they are unearthed while we seek possible sources that may be unknown to us.

Key Chapter Learning

This chapter focused on our access to what is known and what is possible within the parameters of time, financial and human resources, and ethical considerations. We identified probable sources of information and diversity of sources. The research team's access to that information determines the initial scope and potential for a meaningful study. We present a systematic and logical way to review existing knowledge and maximize the use of digital resources. We list steps to search databases with descriptors, utilize existing reference applications to help us reference literature in an easy and effective manner, digitally document unwritten source material, analyze evidence, and synthesize what is known in order to build and write the literature review of a collaborative action research report. Our goal is for the literature review to provide the researcher and the research project authority (as a person who knows), strengthens one's voice, and avoid reinventing what is already known by finding new and refreshing ways, angles to study a challenge.

Essential Questions

What are primary sources of information?
What is peer-review and why is it important?
What are the parts of an original report of a research published in a journal article?

Activity

Conduct a library database search for original research published about the online communication habits among teenagers in the United States and its impact on their academic success. List the steps taken to select the descriptors, determine the terms used to separate the descriptors to reduce or enlarge the number of records, limit the search to journal articles published in the past 5–20 years, and review the abstracts.

Resources

ERIC (eric.ed.gov)—Educational Resources Information Center
Fact Check (www.factcheck.org)—checks the factual accuracy of what is said by major U.S. political players in the form of TV ads, debates, speeches, interviews and news releases.
Hoax Slayer—debunks email and social media hoaxes and educates web users about email, social media, and Internet security issues, since 2003.
PolitiFact (www.politifact.com)—researches statements and rates their accuracy on the Truth-O-Meter, from True to False. The most ridiculous falsehoods get the lowest rating, Pants on Fire.
Snopes (www.snopes.com)—researches and analyzes rumors and provides evidence to confirm or deny, since 1995.
Zotero (www.zotero.com)—maintains a list of references through free online that populates immediately.

Tables to organize the literature:

Table 4.9: Empirical Studies Organizer

Challenge	Purpose of the Study	Population's Features and Sample Profile and Size	Key Findings	Relation of the Study to Our Study
				Make sure in this column to quote verbatim. Make sure to make the connections between quotations and your study.

Source: G. Arriaza and L. Scott © 2020

Table 4.10: Theoretical Studies Organizer

Summary of the Central Theoretical Argument	Challenge Under Discussion	Contribution of Theoretical Argument to Our Study
		Make sure in this column to quote verbatim. Make sure to make the connections between quotations and your study.

Source: G. Arriaza and L. Scott © 2020

Table 4.11: Parts of an Annotated Bibliography

Reference
Concise Description of the Research
Evaluate Author Authority and Point of View

Source: G. Arriaza and L. Scott © 2020

Table 4.12: Mapping the Literature to the Study

My Study's Variables	Match of Article/Book One List of Contributions to My Study's Variables	Match of Article/Book Two "P" Contributions to My Study's Variables
Variable X		
Variable Y		
Variable Z		

Source: G. Arriaza and L. Scott © 2020

References

Ajayi, O. O. (2010). *A review of the current literature, both pro and con, concerning the use of school uniforms.* (Unpublished thesis). University of Georgia, Athens, GA.

Creswell, J. W., & Creswell, J. D. (2017). *Research design: Qualitative, quantitative, and mixed methods approaches.* Los Angeles, CA: Sage.

Hanson, M. (2015, September 28). Littleton High girls call schools' dress codes sexist. *The Lowell Sun.* Retrieved from http://www.lowellsun.com

Hendricks, C. C. (2017). *Improving schools through action research: A reflective practice approach.* Upper Saddle River, NJ: Pearson.

Krathwohl, D. R. (2009). *Methods of educational and social science research: The logic of methods* (3rd ed.). Long Grove, IL: Waveland Press.

McDaniel, T. (2016). Say what? The principal's t-shirt conundrum. *American Secondary Education, 44*(3), 13–18.

Pavlakis, A., & Roegman, R. (2018). How dress codes criminalize males and sexualize females of color. *Phi Delta Kappan, 100*(2), 54–58.

Perrin, R. (2018). *Pocket guide to APA style* (6th ed.). Stamford, CT: Cengage.

Smith, N. (2012). Eliminating gender stereotypes in public school dress codes: The necessity of respecting personal preference. *Journal of Law and Education, 41,* 251.

Sousa, B. J., & Clark, A. M. (2018). Sharing diverse voices: An imperative for qualitative research. *International Journal of Qualitative Methods, 17,* 1–2

Tompkins, G. (2017). *Literacy for the 21st century: A balanced approach* (7th ed.). Boston: Allyn & Bacon.

5

The Method

[T]his research method is a well-suited approach to analyze the concern of power dynamics within the two-way-bilingual-immersion classroom. The principal investigator team sought a research approach – qualitative methods in participatory action research - that is democratic and equitable in nature among all participants: a cadre of eight two-way bilingual immersion teachers from two school districts and the principal investigator team. The participants are stakeholders embedded in the area of concern and have a mutual interest to bring about change [. . .] Throughout the study, this community of eight teachers kept journals. They reflected on the successes and challenges they encountered in their efforts to incorporate culturally responsive teaching strategies. This team met frequently to review the initial study results, studied the literature, shared insights from their struggles and successes and reflected on how, as a collective, they could incorporate the learning into action plans.

Elizabeth Brooke Garza (study report)

This book has covered four essential steps of the collaborative action research methodology thus far. In Chapter One we presented the conceptual framework of collaboration action research design; in Chapter Two we explained the what and how to define a challenge; in Chapter Three we detailed how to formulate the research question, and in Chapter Four we discussed how to review the existing knowledge about the challenge we are investigating. In this chapter we focus on data collection approaches in qualitative studies.

We consider qualitative methods as a key investigative approach suitable for the design of collaborative action research. As researcher Brook Garza states in the vignette above, the use of qualitative methods in collaborative (participatory) action research allows the study of power dynamics within concrete realms, where participants benefit from their insider role while laboring as researchers. This agency opens access to the innermost details of the issue under investigation down to a granular level. She also points out to three fundamental features of the methodology: the constant checking of results, the sharing of new insights, and the translation of the learning into action plans.

Given its malleability, qualitative research allows for easy adaptation to any design of a collaborative (participatory) action research project. While we recognize that two types of data—qualitative and quantitative—and along with them, two types of methodologies have informed the field, we posit though that these, in reality, always go hand in hand.

We have stressed in the previous chapters the mixed methods approach upon which collaborative action research rests. This means that our approach draws on available qualitative and quantitative methods and procedures to collect and analyze any type of evidence. Nonetheless, this chapter centers on the design of qualitative studies. Yet, whether mixed, quantitative, or qualitative method, one determines appropriate to address the needs of a particular study, collaborative action research provides the most reliable framework.

We outlined the framework of collaborative action research's four core components in Chapter One. Let's repeat here only two of them:

1. *The adaptability* of the design—which allows us to bring in tools such as, to name a few: observation, participant observer, interviews, field notes, and journals.
2. *The inferential* nature of the methodology—which makes it possible for us to unearth narratives buried in the margins of predominant discourses.

Throughout the history of qualitative methodology, the exhaustive portrayal of daily experience has been possible due to the documentation of people's lived experiences through, for instance, stories, testimonies, song, poetry, literature, photography, film, painting, and writing. These sources sit at the core of qualitative data. Through qualitative methods, we access the means to collect and study these data and draw some understanding of the challenge we study. Surveys, descriptive and inferential statistics, inventories, census, polls, are all customarily numerical ways to document people's experience too. Data in the form of numbers anchor the basis of quantitative data. Quantitative methodology provides us the means to collect these data, and build some understanding of the challenge we investigate.

We consider numbers as symbolic representations of narratives. They compress large amounts of description, as in the assertions:

> "[I]n this center, more than 50 percent of the effort is carried out by 20 percent of the workforce"; "80 out of every 100 graduates go on to full employment within 2 years after graduation."

Narrating the life experiences lying beneath each number of the individuals included in these hypothetical statements would present a clearer picture, and a much more compelling evidence supporting the case we are trying to make.

Explaining the roots and manifestations of the qualitative and quantitative divide goes far beyond the scope of this book. We want to only stress the existence of both types of data and methodologies. We, again, just want to affirm that we do not need to see the divide as an unsurmountable split. Metrics and descriptions aid each other, complement, and fill in all the spaces depicting the contours, and the texture of our lived experiences. We also now count with the technology that makes it possible to bridge this separation by converting narratives into numbers. In this twenty-first century, we have arrived to a point where said technologic advances allow us to both pursue the qualitative details behind cold numbers and transform into numbers qualitative data. In the absence of a third, inclusive, way of describing them, we will, for clarity purposes, keep calling these types of methodologies and data -qualitative and quantitative.

Features of Qualitative Methodology

Qualitative methodology encompasses a plethora of approaches, such as: ecological psychology, ethno-biography, teacher research, grounded, case, ethnography, critical discourse, and sociolinguistics. Qualitative methodology is used in a variety of fields ranging from anthropology, hermeneutics, sociology, journalism, education, linguistics, legal, and medical studies.

When qualitative methodology is used in collaborative action research, we consider four core distinctive features:

1. Qualitative methodology looks at events taking place at the ground level. These events are usually documented as they occur, and over a sustained period of time. But also, they are recorded as recollections. In the latter case, we reconstruct memory through testimonial accounts of those directly involved, or who bore witness to the occurrences. The principal research team keeps close tabs on both cases—protagonists and witnesses—as a way to fully and authentically capture their experience, and the texture of the event itself. Carefully assembling archival materials and any documentation available affords crucial data as well. To achieve strong data quality, we carefully follow valid and reliable data collection procedures.
2. Qualitative methodology concerns itself with experiences from within (also called emic) an organization. Protagonists and all involved in the actions being documented make the *primary sources* of the documentation process. Life experiences from outside (also called etic) the organization, or *secondary sources*, contribute as corroborating and complementary evidence to the primary sources. The principal research team keeps track of these two sources at all times.
3. Qualitative methodology documents events in a holistic manner, so that to place them within their actual context. Context here refers to the cultural conditions, the social relations, the backgrounds, and political and economic forces at play. Instead of reality's snippets, this contextualizing helps picture whole realities. The principal research team counts on this context to position the event within its own environment, and that way to more accurately portray it and build reliable understanding. Then, explaining the phenomenon under study becomes fully possible.
4. Qualitative methodology pays careful attention to bias throughout the entire planning, execution, and analysis and interpretation of the collected evidence. As we discussed this issue in Chapter One, bias lies in wait at all times and represents a serious validity and reliability threat in collaborative action research. The native condition of the principal research team and all research collaborators may erase the necessary distance one needs from the issue under study. Hence, heightened recognition of our proclivities and assumed understandings throughout the research process, is a must. Go back to Chapter One for bias control recommendations.

We follow these four features very closely when designing and implementing a qualitative study. We infuse every single step of the design and implementation process with each of them, and pay special attention to the adaptability and the inferential, grounds-up nature of collaborative action research. Data collection approaches, and the instruments applied, are of vital importance to qualitative studies. In the following section, we detail some salient features.

Data Strength

The success of a research project hinges on its credibility. We build credibility throughout the study's entire design and implementation. Validity and reliability sit at the core of this preoccupation. To achieve strong data quality, we need to make four methodological considerations—ensure data's veracity, confirm that the sample truly represents the population, establish clear boundaries of the data, and recognize limitations of the study.

Data Veracity: We consider veracity as a two-parallel-tracks process. On one track, we must ensure that any data collection instrument used in our study can actually be applied by others to similar studies; on the other track we must ensure that any data collected authentically mirror the reality we intended to document. In order to succeed implementing this double process, we must pay attention to the following work areas:

1. *Data Triangulation:* We seek at least three different data points to corroborate authenticity. In her team study, researcher Brook-Garza explains that to ensure the "trustworthiness of my data and findings I triangulated the data through classroom observation, member checking, and external audit." The author tells about her intentional checking of data across three areas: data collected through observations; team members checking the accuracy of transcriptions and findings; and non-team members auditing data sets.

    Triangulation means searching for data we collect on an item, or sets of items, in different places such as archival documentation, interview transcripts, and surveys. When checking these, sources go examine those items we have determined to be of great importance to the study. If the study, for example, looks at allocation of resources dealing with environmental sustainability, we may check budgeting policy, accounting procedures, and selection criteria for the allocation of said resources.

We can also triangulate participant's responses within an instrument. We can do this by asking the same question on an item using different wording. The decision to double check the accuracy of responses to an item depends on the importance we attribute to said item, and whether the item lends itself for confusion. We may also ask the same exact question in different instruments.

2. *Data Collection Process:* It maps out the step-by-step actions we foresee taking to gather data. As in any road map, these procedures indicate the general direction we want to take, and do not provide detailed description of each of the steps. Yet, we adhere and keep close control of the procedures, because as it happens when following a road map, not doing so may lead us to nowhere, and to the loss of time and resources. The principal research team establishes ways to introduce modifications to the original map, as well as ways to check their implementation.

While we cannot prescribe anything a priori, we consider data collection procedures must follow this principle: *the nature of the challenge, the study design, the research question, and data collection procedures must all coherently fit together*.

Nonetheless, when planning we need to consider these points.

1. Individual interviews, in general, let us produce detailed data, but they may be time consuming. Plan them as a way to create focus groups.
2. Focus groups, in general, save time and produce useful data, but not necessarily at a granular level. They may help us identify individuals we may want to follow up later. The interviewer needs some experience conducting these type of interviews to maximize quantity and quality of data.
3. In-depth interviews allow us to collect granular and private level data. We can also check data collected from previous efforts, such as from individual and focus groups.
4. Observations facilitate access to new data, corroborate previously collected data, and may be implemented at any stage of the study's procedures.
5. Shadowing helps us to corroborate data, and to get as close as possible to real-life experiences as lived by the individual or groups we follow.

In our Brook-Garza team study example, the principal research team established a multi-layered data collection process involving two phases:

Phase One:
(a) First interview: the researcher sought for interviewees to describe their background, experiences, attitudes, and practices they use to promote equitable linguistic and social interactions.
(b) Focus groups interviews: the researcher defined these as "communities of inquiry." Interviews were embedded with readings intended to promote reflection and discussion. "We reviewed the research describing the fundamental concepts of two-way immersion programs, power imbalances, culturally responsive pedagogy, and equitable spaces. The focus group then reflected and discussed which practices promoted cultural competency." Participants kept a daily journal to track their experiences in the classroom.
(c) Final interview: At the end of the study's cycle, the author interviewed participants individually. She sought to document whether participants "experienced any change or transformation in their description of awareness, attitudes, and practice."
(d) Classroom observations: These were implemented throughout the entire study and aimed at gathering data on how strategies discussed during focus groups were implemented by all participants. These were "holistic observations of teacher practices, student participation, use of language, discourse, and classroom dynamics."

Phase Two:
(a) Validity checking: After all data were transcribed, the team checked the text for accuracy, ask other participants to double check said text. The draft report was examined by all participants to establish its legitimacy. The team then employed an external audit procedure by having two teachers who were not participants read the report and offer final feedback.

3. *Data as a Learning Catalytic:* We research what we do not know. As we have said in previous chapters, a core purpose of collaborative action research involves learning. This is so because the adaptability of collaborative action research makes it possible for a research team and its community to interact with the challenge under study and its surrounding social and cultural context. In addition, this very dynamic becomes a reliable source of information, ideas, opinions on the study's procedures, methods, and technologies. Educating ourselves while researching requires a very purposeful plan. In collaborative action research learning takes place, as we just stated, at two distinctive levels.

1. We learn about the issue(s) we are investigating. From the very initial stages of challenge identification, we launch an effort to discover its sources, multiple manifestations, and ramifications. We also study the available knowledge about it, and search for the internal conditions that may help explain the challenge's significance. We also consider larger, external forces at play, and which may help us understand the larger context.
2. Capacity building embedded in the planning and executing a collaborative action research may occur provided we plan for it. Team members, and the community at large, expose themselves to the different stages of a project: from problem identification techniques, the design of a study, the mapping of the procedures, and the data collection and analysis technologies.

Population and Sample: Population here only means people. We consider population and its representation—the sample—a core component of the research plan. We first need to have a clear identification of the population, and then a precise boundary. Identifying a population involves an intentional selection of who we want to include in our study. In order to do this, we must set unambiguous selection criteria to guide each step of the effort.

1. We first ground the selection of *who* we want to research, on the study's *purpose and question.*
   In our example, Brook-Garza research team sought "to examine (a) teacher understanding of cross-cultural competence, (b) teacher awareness of power imbalance regarding the validation of cultural capital between native English-speakers and native Spanish-speakers, and (c) the teacher organizational routines that lead to equitable distribution of cultural capital in their classrooms."
   The team wanted to answer: What practices do teachers use to promote cross-cultural competency in the two-way bilingual immersion (TWBI) classroom?
2. Then, we consider the population's features—e.g., age, gender, formal education, roles, and functions.
   In our example, the team wanted to study (a) bilingual education teachers, (b) elementary and middle schools.
3. Third, we can only study individuals and groups we have uncomplicated access. Collaborative action research typically involves populations from

our own organization, thus easily accessible. In our sample, the team selected population members who were interested in participating, and willing to add to their schedules the study's work requirements, and time.
4. Fourth, we bound the population. Bounding the population here means creating explicit borders to isolate the targeted population from others. For instance, in our sample study the teacher population included all bilingual programs of a school district that counts five bilingual programs across nine elementary and three middle schools. The Brook-Garza team bounded the population by including only dual-immersion programs.
5. Fifth, we now are ready to select our sample. Establishing a set of criteria is of vital importance. These criteria include concrete features tied to the study's purpose and question. In our sample, the team determined the following: (a) participants identified themselves as two-way immersion teachers in a program self-described as following the two-way immersion model; (b) the participants were either presently fourth through sixth grade two-way immersion teachers or the teachers had previously taught fourth through sixth grade two-way immersion classes; (c) participants exhibited a desire to form a community of inquiry and action research.
6. Sixth, once we establish the selection criteria, we choose participants. Picking a sample in collaborative action research may follow a randomized or a non-randomized procedure. Randomized sampling makes the opportunity to be selected equal to all members of a population. Non-randomized sampling tends to follow a convenience or networking connections procedure. We recommend either of the two approaches below or a combination of both:

   (a) *Convenient sampling (non-randomized):* This approach draws on participants' social networks. We ask individuals readily available and willing to participate in our study. Studying our own institutions makes it feasible to recruit participants we know. We invite those who fit our criteria and, either we keep recruiting more participants, or invite the individuals we asked already to help us identify and recruit others they know fit our selection criteria. The selection process occurs naturally. While still meeting the selection criteria, choosing biased individuals represents the approach's greatest risk. Brook Garza tells us the process. She reached out a group of colleagues from "a different school site from my own, [who] were approached during informal conversations the school year prior to the start of the study. I also asked a friend and former colleague who is now teaching at Vineyard

Valley Joint Unified School District if she was interested in participating." From this initial group, the snowballing effect started. The researcher continues, referring to the last colleague she approached: "She, in turn, stated that a couple of her colleagues at her school site were also interested in participating."

(b) *Quota sampling (randomized):* This is a methodical and multilayered approach that looks for the representation of the different groups that make up a population. First, based on reliable demographic information (e.g., the most recent census), the population is split into its different social groups. Second, according to each of the groups' size, establish their proportional representation. For example, all teachers in a K-8 school divided by grade level: early grades (K-third grade), middle grades (fourth to sixth grade), and upper grades (seventh and eighth grades). Third, determine the most salient features for the sample representing the population, such as gender, race, ethnicity, age, expertise, and job description. Fourth, apply a simple random process to select individuals. For instance, using a computer application assign a number to each individual, then choose only those whose number is a multiple of, say, five.

Study Limitations: As we mentioned earlier in this book, a unit of analysis refers to the number of participants in a study. It can also be an organizational entity, such as a school, or group of schools, a classroom, or set of classrooms. A unit of analysis in a Collaborative action research project typically comprises one's own institution, and a small group of individuals or organizational entity, such as a set of classrooms. Limitations mean that, from the very inception of a study, a team acknowledges its constraints. Namely, the findings emerging from a study only apply to the unit of analysis involved, and indirectly to the rest of the organization. Hence, it is a good practice that a report always contains a section specifying these borders.

Generalization refers to outspreading the findings to the programs, or populations reflected in the sample. Claims, therefore, hold a powerful value relative to such environment. Consequently, claiming something else may amount to a lack of professional honesty. The potential transformative power of collaborative action research resides precisely on the fact that it affords a granular level analysis. It can illuminate other challenges afflicting the organization, and help find solutions at the local level.

Furthermore, findings and understandings from a particular collaborative action research may serve as guidance to studies in places with similar circumstances and conditions. Thus, in these cases replicating a study may be restricted to data collection techniques, instrumentation, and the main components of the design.

Data Collection and Organization

We organize what we collect. The usefulness of the evidence certainly depends on the meticulous organization we followed when gathering it. Every single piece of data must be organized at the same time. Selection of both, the approach and the instruments, hinges on the type of challenge we want to research. In Chapter Three we reviewed how to differentiate the variables, how to break these down into factors, and how to identify the components of a factor, which are called *items*. We stated that an item indicates how the challenge expresses itself in the reality under study. After we have created our items, we can say that we are ready to develop our instrument's questions.

We consider next four of the most relevant approaches to collect qualitative evidence: observation, participant observer, interviews, and shadowing. We also outline the instruments that best fit each approach. These include field notes, observation protocols, journals, and questionnaires. Along with each of these, we offer various types of organizing templates.

Observation

Looking attentively at concrete events as they develop, so that to capture every single detail of it, summarizes this simplest and oldest way to know about our existence and the environment around us. Through all of our senses we feel, capture, process analytically, and learn critically about experience and, ultimately, enrich our knowledge. As a method, researchers have over time learned to sharpen this natural capacity to observe.

Principal research teams do observe purposefully, meticulously, and truthfully. Each second observed counts. Capturing all the particulars of what is being observed require good note-taking, and close attention to every single aspect of the event being observed. Observation takes place in a concrete physical area, such as a classroom, a building, a town's central square, a ward. We seek to observe in the most unobtrusive manner possible. At the same time that we become invisible to participants, they continue their routine naturally, yielding authentic data to our study.

Observation needs to follow tight protocols delineating clear and laser-focused procedures.

Observation Protocol consists of goals, procedures, and ethical considerations. Once the principal research team agrees on these points, they negotiate meanings, and proactively share them with participants. A study's significance depends on participants' involvement. They and the principal research team, in our collaborative action research model, co-produce the knowledge that emanates from the practices being observed. This conscientious contribution promotes ownership of both the process and the products.

Goals: Participants' main contact, such as a classroom teacher (who, ideally would be a member of the principal research team or of a research support team), must contribute to and agree with the delineated purposes of the study, and the goals for each of the observations. The goals and objectives of an observation must be clearly articulated and explained at every opportunity.

A goal answers this question: What do we want to get out of this observation?

Data needs, generated by the ground-level questions, determine the observation goals, session by session (see more about ground-level questions below, under "interviews," and also check the research question in Chapter Three).

Procedures: Observer and participants' main contact must have an understanding of at least the following issues:

- o What will be observed?
- o Who will be observed?
- o Who will observe?
- o When is the starting and ending time?
- o How will the observation be recorded?
- o Where is the observation point?

The main contact also needs to be aware of the typical steps of an observation. See the steps' outline immediately after the point on ethics.

Ethics: All the appropriate steps to protect vulnerable populations must be taken care of prior to any observation. Most institutions have established an institutional review board (IRB), or its equivalent, as an internal body to approve and monitor research projects. Here we list key areas to consider:

- o Obtain consent by the organization's administration.
- o Collect consent by participants.
- o Define clearly who will read and hear the recorded data.
- o Establish how the participants' identity will be protected, especially that of vulnerable populations, such as children.
- o Determine where all collected data will be concentrated and for how long.

Observation Steps

Pre: Aims at establishing rapport and earning trust between observer and observed. Rapport and trust must be considered as on-going processes. They cannot be taken for granted. The research team starts by taking care of any power imbalance that may exist between participants and the observer. This is particularly crucial when the observer holds hierarchical authority over the participants. Observing does not, and can never, serve the institution's evaluative needs. If this imbalance cannot be solved, especially due to skepticism, or mistrust, the observation then must be conducted by a person who does not embody hierarchical authority. We want participants to understand that the research for which we collect data via observations holds something beneficial to them.

In sum, the pre-observation work must:

- ❖ Establish strong rapport that yields unrestricted access to the observer.
- ❖ Build trust around power imbalances and the study's purposes, so that the observation affords authentic data.
- ❖ Inculcate participants' sense of ownership of the research process and thus strengthen mutual trust.
- ❖ Have precise goals for each observation.
- ❖ Execute every observation in the most inconspicuous way possible.
- ❖ Check the technology intended to record data works fine.

Through: Seeks to execute each observation as carefully as possible. Make sure again that all technical equipment is fully operational. Set this equipment in places where participants will not notice, or will quickly ignore it. The observer must find a location from which to watch unobtrusively. The observer systematically follows, point by point, the observation protocol.

We highly recommend that, even when recording each observation, the observer takes hand written profuse and clear field notes.

After: Pursues precision and clarity. Express thanks to the participants and promise to come back later. Share notes with the main contact person. Make sure the contact person knows the observation goals and the study's purposes, and is a full participant. Share the collected data, it helps to double-check their veracity, identify data holes, and challenges.

Participant Observer

When the observer joins in the action being studied, the roles of researcher and participant become one. The researcher acts on the very issue under investigation, while at the same time documents both the actions as well as their impact, like an actor documenting the audience's reactions to the play, while at the same time she is recording her own acting.

The adaptability of collaborative action research requires constant sharing of both the data and the preliminary results. The assumption here is that doing so may allow for modifications to the action itself, and to the methodology and, that way, improve the end results. Such flexibility offers great strength to the method, but it also poses its greatest threat—exerting influence on the research project. Using participant observer as a key way to collect data, therefore, makes bias an even greater threat. As a consequence, such double-function requires a high bias awareness from the principal research team.

On the one hand, the observer must keep personal opinions and preferences on constant check, and must also ensure fidelity to the goals of the observation and to the purposes and question of the research project. The latter two—purpose and question—ultimately lead every aspect of the research. On the other hand, recording the details of the action must follow faithful description.

Controlling bias increases rigor, and to achieve this we recommend:

1. Immediately after an observation happens, the participant observer must take handwritten or typed notes. In order to do so, the participant observer can help the effort by imbuing the habit of quick-writes. These short, on the fly, annotations become quite useful as they may aid triggering fresh memory of the event being recorded.
2. A secondary observer—such as a member of the principal research or a support team—could also witness and take notes to aid the participant observer to reconstruct any missing part of the documented event.
3. Videotaping and sound recording of the action will be extremely useful to corroborate the participant observer's field notes.

Field Notes

The three recommendations above—quick-writes, second observer, videotaping, plus strong bias control—can be of great help for our full accounts of the lived experience. As we have stated, writing down a narrative of what we observe is indispensable in qualitative studies, and whether as participant observer, or just as observer, this writing describes our direct contact with what occurred. Our means to do so is field notes. Field notes simply trace the unfolding story of an action. Field notes do not contain our own ideas, feelings, or positions.

Field notes account for what happens to others. They contain what we see occurring, in real time, to the participants in the action.

The challenge presented by taking field notes at the same time that the observer participates in the action may be overcome by habitually dividing the field notes writing into two moments:

> First simply jot down short descriptions of key moments during the action. We have also called this activity quick-writes. Using key words, phrases, and short sentences will do it.
>
> Second, after each observation the observer must block some time to craft full narratives, and follow the quick-writes as triggers to fill in the data.

A field note template contains the following (see Table 5.1 below).

- ❖ Date
- ❖ Place
- ❖ Participants
- ❖ Observer
- ❖ Observation goal
- ❖ Starting time
- ❖ Ending time

Table 5.1: Observation Template

Participants	Observation

Source: G. Arriaza. © 2020

Field notes, we insist, must accurately mirror what occurred. The value of our data depends on the degree the field notes exactly capture the events we attempted to record. This assertion leads us to this point: the observer strictly reports what was observed. Personal feelings, thoughts, and any type of personal reaction must not appear on the field notes. The observer, nonetheless, may choose to do two things:

1. *Keep a journal* to track all personal annotations. Journaling, as a research practice, should be considered an important complementary data source. A journal tracks what happens to us, the participant observer, at the personal and professional levels. Due to the fact that collaborative action research teams belong to the organization under study, their members should be considered study participants in general, and chiefly when they act as participant observer. We consider journaling as a reflective moment that occurs *after* completing the field notes.
2. *Write memos to yourself.* A memo attempts to capture fleeting thoughts, instinctive reactions when observing an action. Recording those instantaneous and short-lived experiences eventually serve as data source. When, indeed, the research team examines the evidence and begins to make some sense out of it, having those short annotations will definitely help. When memoing, make sure to stay within the realm of what is *felt or thought in the moment*. Leave any rational, analytical thinking, to journaling. Memoing occurs at specific moments only, not necessarily throughout an observation. See Table 5.2 below.

Table 5.2: Observation and Memo Template

Participants Observation	Memo

Source: G. Arriaza © 2020

Field notes sample:
Melissa Reese, a classroom teacher leader, embarked in a collaborative study at her site. The study aimed at producing better understanding about the different literacy programs, and classroom instruction. The research project pursued this question: How do lower elementary school children decipher reading content?

Note that the researchers collected two types of details:

(a) Oral communication between Mrs. Bee. and the students. The dialogue was recorded verbatim, exactly as it ensued. The researcher used quotation marks to separate this talk from the other observation.
(b) The surrounding context of the oral communication. The observer took careful detailed notes of movement, place, and side-talk. The researcher placed these data in brackets to distinguish it from the oral communication.

Date: March 15, 2020
Place: MLK Elementary School, 2nd Grade Classroom
Participants: Mrs. Bee (2nd Grade General Ed Teacher) and 13 Male, 12 Female Students (2nd Grade)
Observer: Melissa Reese
Observation focus: Whole Group Language Arts Instruction
Starting time: 10:16
Ending time: 10:54

Participants	Observation
Mrs. Bee	[Teacher is sitting at a chair while students are sitting criss-cross at the carpet in no particular order. Teacher is holding up a card with a word and a picture on it]. "Our next word is 'defeat'. What is defeat?" [Nods at student raising his hand].
Male student 1	"For example, U.S. won against Belgium so U.S. defeated Belgium." [Another male student starts speaking]
Male student 2	"I defeated them. It means you lose."
Mrs. Bee	"I like it. Alright, defeat means to win a victory over someone in a battle or contest" [Teacher stops and quietly talks to a student] "Are you chewing gum? I hope you're not chewing gum. We already went over this. Whatever is in your mouth, please throw it away." [Student gets up and walks quietly to the trash can to throw something away. Some students turn to look, but the teacher is moving quickly on with the lesson]. "Another vocabulary word this week is 'worry'. What does that mean?" [Makes eye contact to acknowledge female student raising her hand]
Female student3	'Worry' is like when you get lost. You get sad."
Male student 3	[Student speaks without being called on], "My mom always worries."
Mrs. Bee	"Good. Worry means to feel uneasy or uncertain about what will happen. Our next word is 'code'."
Male student 1	"Ummm...something in a box, you need a code."
Mrs. Bee	"Oh, right. Like with our chrome book cart. We put in a code to open it and get the chrome books. This kind of code means there is a set of laws or rules about how to behave. That's what this kind of code means. Code is a multiple meaning word."
Male student 2	[Speaks without being called on], "like my video game, I need to put in a code to unlock the next level."
Mrs. Bee	[Teacher moves on without acknowledging student's statement]. "Our last word is 'eager'."

Participants	Observation
Female student 5	"Like happy to do something."
Female student 3	"Curious"
Female student 5	"Excited"
Ms. Bee	[Teacher responds while getting out a book. No eye contact]. "About 4 weeks this time. Bruce, Valerie, Kenny..." [Teacher places checks next to their names being projected on the whiteboard]. "Thank you to those who have their book and reading companions out." [Teacher looks around the room at students. Students are all sitting at desk, the room is quiet, and students are at various stages of following the directions]. "Here, this is extra." [He hands paper to the teacher, who takes it and smiles. He sits back down]. "OK, does everyone have a reading companion? OK, what is the standard?"
Female student 6	"RL2.5"
Mrs. Bee	"RL2.5. Remember the 2 is 2nd grade and the 5 tells us that we are working on Beginning, middle, and end. That's what we are working on this week with George Washington." [Teacher scans the room with her eyes while speaking. The majority of children are looking at their books while only six are making eye contact with the teacher while she speaks].
Male student 4	"Page 30?"
Mrs. Bee	"Yes, page 30. Alright, I'll let you use pen or highlighter for annotating."
Males student 1	"Can I use pencil?"
Males student 3	"Can I use more than one?"
Ms. Bee	"No, pick one." Teacher projects story while students get out pens. "OK, we are on page 30. Can you remind me who George Washington is?" [Teacher nods at student raising his hand].

Participants	Observation
Female student 6	"He was our first president."
Ms Bee	"What else did we learn about Washington?"
Several students	"We learned he asked Betsy Ross to make our battle flag."
Ms. Bee	"Right."
Female student 5	"I know lots of facts."
Ms. Bee	"Oh, you know lots of facts?" [Random students start chatting in the room]. "OK, we need to remember when someone is talking we need to be listening because they're going to say something we need to know. OK, remember you only need one pen to annotate." [Teacher plays story and shows on projector. Students following along on screen and books. Teacher walks room. Whispers to student. Teacher walks to the front of the room and watches the screen]. "Alright, don't turn the page yet. Who's this in the picture?"
Female student 6	"Benjamin Franklin."
Ms. Bee Female student 6	"Right. Do you remember what we learned about him?" "yes"
Male student 2	"No. When?"
Ms. Bee	"Remember when I made the poster?"
Male student 2	"Oh, yeah."
Ms. Bee	"Any key details yet?"
Male student 5	"The war is not going well."
Ms. Bee	"Where did you find that?"
Male student 6	"Page 6."
Ms. Bee	"Good. This tells us we might lose the war. OK, anymore?" "The 13 colonies in paragraph 7."
Female student 3	"Why is that important?"

Participants	Observation
Ms. Bee	"Because if we didn't have 13 colonies, we wouldn't have any people." "OK, why else, Walker, were the 13 colonies important?" [Teacher calls on student that is looking inside their desk and doing something with their hands].
Male student 1 Ms. Bee	"I wasn't thinking that." "What were you thinking?"
Male student 1	"Nothing."
Ms. Bee	"OK, well... I am asking, why were the 13 colonies important?" [Silent pause]. "Do you want to tell me?"
Male student 1	"No."
Ms. Bee	"OK." [Calls on another student].
Male student 4	"I think part of America was like England."
Male student 1	"Anything else you want to highlight?"
Ms. Bee	"Paragraph 8 in 11/2 years they lost wars"
Female student 3	"Did they tell us there is a problem?"
Ms. Bee	"Yes."
Female student 3	"Where?"
Ms. Bee	"Right there. It says we have a problem.
Female student 3	"Right. OK. Who are the main characters?"
Random student	"Ben and Tom."
Ms. Bee	"OK. Write Tom and Franklin. These are our main characters" [Teacher writes this on the board for students to copy. They copy it].
Male student 6	"Are we going to learn about Elon Musk soon?"
Ms. Bee	[Teacher giggles]. "OK, are we all on page 32?" [Teacher plays story on projector and walks to back of the room. Pauses story]. "Even though Tom is just a boy, do you think he can deliver this letter?"

Participants	Observation
Male student 2	"Yes."
Mrs. Bee	"Does Franklin think he can?"
Male student 7	"No, it's too dangerous."
Ms. Bee	"He's only 12."
Male student 8	"He can go to jail."
Mrs. Bee	"Do you think since you're just a kid someone would just let you go?"
Male student 5	"Yes."
Ms. Bee	"Yes. So, if you're a kid and you look like you're up to no good, do you think the police would stop you or question you or let you go?"
Female student 3	"Question you."
Ms. Bee	[Teacher points to the map]. "This is where the enemy is."
Random student	"Nooo, the enemy is on the other side Mrs. B."
Ms. Bee	"Is it? No. Wait. OK. Let me see. Let me think." [Giggles]. "OK, you're right. Sorry guys. So the enemy is here and he needs to go all this way and cross the river at night." [Students look on the map on the screen and in books. Teacher looks at the time]. "OK, leave this where it is. Let's go to lunch." [Teacher and students start to walk out the door. Soft student chatter takes place as they exit].

Source: Melissa Reese, literacy observations, 2019.

Interviews

An interview is an intentional conversation, and not an interrogation. Interviews are steered by the research question. They help us in our attempts to gain a good understanding of our participants' life experiences, thoughts, and feelings. An interview may easily generate an instant relationship between the two parties. Whether an interview with an individual or with a focus group, the interviewer strives to put the respondent at ease, and create an atmosphere of mutual respect. In the context of a collaborative action research, add trust to both easiness and respect. We can build trust with respondents by facilitating their understanding of their answers' value, and the benefits their voluntary involvement may bring to them and the institution.

The questionnaire is the key instrument. Two essential considerations follow:

First, when creating a data collection instrument, we pay close attention to: (a) *consistency*—how the instrument treats the issue throughout; and (b) *meaning*—how the questions denote the same thing to all participants. We want an instrument that collects the data we intend. The stronger the consistency (i.e., reliability) and meaning (i.e., validity) of an instrument, the more likely it can be replicated in a study looking at the same issue, in a different place, a similar population, and circumstances alike to the ones of the original study.

Second, the crafting of good instruments depends on this understanding: data quality is as good as our instruments. We need to have clear understanding of the participants' linguistic, cultural, and social background and context. It helps us avoid infringing other people's beliefs, values, habits, and mores. Being responsive and honestly respectful to these topics only strengthen the ownership, and usefulness of an instrument.

After we have carefully considered the points above, we are ready to move on to itemizing. To do so, please go back to Chapter Three where we detailed the step-by-step process of how to break a research question down to its most minuscule parts—the items. After you do go back to Chapter Three, come here again to consider a few greatly important issues when creating your questionnaire. In the following sections, we explain the wording and types of questions, and piloting the questionnaire.

Wording Questions

In order for an interview to collect genuine and usable data, whether it is conducted with an individual or a focus group, the interviewer wants to put the responder at easy, lower anxiety or, preempt any kind of concern. This process starts with the formulation of the question. We ought to decide the wording and the type of questions. As interviewers we check each question against these points:

(a) Assumes equal cultural decoding between the responder and the question's vocabulary (e.g., What was the most important feature of the program?);
(b) Singularizes the problem by taking an item at a time; uses examples to illustrate meanings;
(c) Role playing and simulation offers cues through context (e.g., Suppose I'm new in this program, what should I know to do well here?);
(d) Disassociate yourself from question (e.g., Assume I . . .?); (e) prefatory statements (Always alert interviewee what is going to happen); (f) summarize and transition (e.g., Now, we've been talking . . . the next questions will . . .).

Types of Questions

The following is a list of most commonly used:

1. *Clarifying:* (e.g., What do you mean by "participatory?)
2. *Probing:* (e.g., What organizational consequences a participatory pedagogy may have at your site?)
3. *Opinion:* (e.g., What's your take on . . .?)
4. *Values:* (e.g., What would you like to see happen?)
5. *Experience:* (e.g., If I follow you around in a typical day, what would I see?)
6. *Behavior:* (e.g., What dressing expectations you have?)
7. *Feeling:* (e.g., How was it for you? How does this make you feel?)
8. *Knowledge:* (e.g., How this situation unfolded?)
9. *Sensory:* Identify participants' sensorial experience (e.g., What did she actually say?)
10. *Background:* Personal or collective history (e.g., Where did you attend before attending this place?)
11. *Demographic:* Identifying characteristics of interviewee (e.g., How do you define yourself?)

Piloting the Questionnaire

As a practice, make sure to try your questionnaire out with a small group of colleagues, and an equally small sample of the target population. At the end of each interview debrief with participants about their experience, and the topics covered. This debriefing should enhance both the instrument and the ways the interviews are being conducted. Until then the questionnaire may be ready for use.

Now you are ready to start an interview cycle.

Varieties of Interviews

After producing the questionnaire, we need now to determine the type of interview, or series of interviews, we want to conduct. We distinguish four types of interviews: structured, semi-structured, unstructured, and in-depth.

Structured Interviews: The interviewer follows systematically the exact list of questions from the questionnaire. Also, the questions are presented in such a way that do not allow the responder to diverge from the interview's core content. A combination of closed questions helps the interview to stay tethered to the goals and purpose of the research project.

Semi-Structured Interviews. The interviewer follows the list of questions from the questionnaire, but allows the responder to branch away from the core content. Letting to branch away may afford angles, perspectives, and new unsuspected areas to surface. At the moment of the interview, keeping track of these emerging points may be difficult to document and follow up, and it also may present a challenge to our efforts collecting data within schedule. Sharp, focused open-ended questions may help diminish the risk of wide branching out. We can pose this this questions easily by carefully itemizing the factors of our research question.

Unstructured Interviews. The interviewer loosely follows the questions from the questionnaire, which becomes more of a guideline. Open-ended questions are preferred, and the interviewer allows the responder to branch away from core content. These interviews may also be considered conversational interviews where the interviewer is more interested in covering the questionnaire's content, than with addressing each and every questions. Allowing the respondent to branch out too widely may be risky in terms of coverage and time. But, as with semi-structured interviews, careful itemizing will help sharpen our questions, and therefore limit the risk.

In-Depth Interviews: The interviewer systematically follows the interviewee through a series of sequential interviews. In-depth means our dedicated effort to obtain all possible specifics of events as lived by participants. We track the content of every response so to follow them all up in the coming interviews, hence the sequential nature of these kind of interviews. As we collect data, we can compare concrete details to previous answers, triangulate with other information sources, and elicit issues raised over the course of the interviews. Unstructured type of interviews and open-ended questions offer the best vehicles to have a continuous interviewing relationship with participants. At the end of these interviews, we should have rich, detailed information on the issue we investigate.

Conducting the Interview

At this point, we have created the questionnaire, identified the participants, decided who we will interview individually, and who in a focus group. We have also double-checked that the technology we plan to use for recording works fine. Now, we finally have arrived to the moment we have been preparing for—executing our interview plan. Conducting the interview includes three distinguishable moments: beginning, developing, and ending.

Beginning the Interview: Start by making sure you build at all times rapport with each participant (thank participants for their time and support, make introductions, and keep time), explain again goals of interview. The more extended this rapport better the chances participants will be at easy with the questions. Do not take initial rapport for granted, though. Check participants are actively engaged. Start with easy-to-answer questions

Developing the Interview: Make sure respondents do not deviate too far from the stem question. Combine different type of questions (e.g., clarifying, probing, knowledge, and feeling). Close one set of questions and introduce another one. Check how respondents are doing.

Ending the Interview: Put clear closure to the entire interview. Check with participants how the experience went. Make appointments for the next interview.

Checking-in with Yourself: After all interviewees have gone, go over your interview questionnaire, and any protocols you created to ensure you asked the questions you needed to ask, list the ones you could not ask, any emerging concerns about participants, items that need further exploration. Journaling about the experience itself, your own reflections, and any concerns is, as we have stated throughout this chapter, a good practice.

Shadowing

Shadowing, as a tool to collect data, may reveal granular details around vital areas, such as habits, time use, priorities, attention, tone, and type of social interactions. The researcher documents actions in real time. Using a pre-agreed protocol, we follow as a shadow the targeted person, taking detailed notes of each occurrence, or the agreed aspects of it.

Shadowing can serve as one more point of evidence for triangulation. The data collected this way may help us double or triple check the degree of veracity of a data set collected by other means, through interviews, for instance. When we want to use shadowing as triangulation, we then must purposefully include in the protocol, the goals of the specific items we need to double check.

Another use of shadowing data is perspective. The intimate, close up view these data affords us provides a different angle from which to observe the issue under study. In this manner, we add a new, often surprising viewpoint, to the data collected somewhere else.

Prior to following the person or group, we must first agree on the purpose of the shadowing, the actual activity to be documented, and the procedures to share and debrief the collected data. A shadowing protocol contains:

1. Place
2. Date
3. Participants
4. Goals
5. Activity
6. Starting and ending time

Table 5.3: Shadowing Field Notes

Participants	Event	Time Used

Source G. Arriaza © 2020

Debriefing: While these data form part of a larger research effort, the iterative nature of collaborative action research requires constant comparison. The debrief is a data-sharing instant. Remember: the principal research team and the study's participants co-construct the research project, the data goals, procedures, and interpretation. Thus, a shadow-debriefing serves as a coaching moment between the principal research team and the participants, to examine the issues the data exposed. For instance, if the goal was to document how time is prioritized by observing the amounts of minutes the participant used dealing with issues, we may show first the raw data recorded using the template in Table 5.3.

But then we may want to present a summary (see Table 5.4 below) of these data tabulated. Here is an example after shadowing a school principal for two hours:

Table 5.4: Shadowing Summary

Event	Time in Minutes
Dealing with teacher-student conflict	25
Responding to central administration	50
Curriculum issues	10
Talking to teachers	5
Talking to office staff: Secretary 10 Counselor 20	30
Total Time	120

Source: G. Arriaza © 2020

Debriefing these data may represent another opportunity to collect more—document the debriefing itself.

Coaching questions could include: What does these data tell you about time use? What does this time investment tell you about your priorities? Is this time use a habit? In what ways can it be modified?

But if shadowing is not meant for coaching participants, then the data can simply be passed around to the participants.

We have outlined core methodological approaches for the collection of qualitative data. Now that we have collected abundant qualitative data, what do we do? In the next chapter, we outline the fundamental procedures of the two steps that follow data gathering—data analysis, and reporting results.

Key Chapter Learning

This chapter first defined qualitative methodology as one that fits well with collaborative action research. Qualitative methodology makes it possible to document participants' lived experiences as these occur. It makes data available at the granular level, and brings to the fore the actual texture of narratives otherwise marginalized. This methodology privileges the inside, bottom up, and inductive data collection. The ever-presence threat of bias inherent to collaborative action research can be controlled and diminished by the holistic nature of qualitative methods, but especially by our careful attention to both our data veracity procedures, and to the selection of the population's sample.

Additionally, the chapter delineated four core qualitative data collection procedures and instruments. We outlined the concept, protocols, habits, and templates of participant observer, observation, interview, and shadowing. Journaling, memoing, quick notes, and how to increase validity and reliability are central points running throughout these four data collection approaches.

Essential Question

How do you reconcile the fact that collecting data from ordinary activities may imply documenting the lived experience of the research team itself?

Activity

Read at least twice the brief case below. Look for patterns. Then do a manual analysis of the case by:

1. Creating a code key.
2. Applying your codes to the observation data. Be open to modify the code key whether deleting the ones you find do not fit to the case, or creating new ones.
3. Grouping codes, once you exhausted the entire text.
4. Creating categories from the groups.
5. Keeping writing memos to yourself throughout the entire activity.
6. Going beyond categories, if need be.

Pioneer View Elementary Case

Pioneer View Elementary School is one of twenty-one public elementary schools in Pioneerland School District which serves a total of 22,376 students in elementary and junior high school grades. Our school is located in an unincorporated section of Pioneer city, and serves students from transitional kindergarten to sixth grade. The city has been identified as one of the most ethnically and linguistically diverse in the nation. According to the unified school data center, Pioneer View enrolled 549 students this year.

    According to the data center, our school demographics show 53% Latinx, 20.2% African American, 6.4% White, 5.1% Asian, 3.8% Filipino, 2.9% Pacific Islander, 8.2% Two or More Races, 0.2% American Indian. In addition, the teacher demographics show a 6% Latinx, 3% African American, 3% Filipino, 6% Asian, 76% White, and 3% No response. The school district data center identifies 131 students as dual English language learners (ELLs). In addition, English

Language Arts (ELA Summative report) reveal 39% of Fairview students (3rd–6th grade) met or exceeded the standard, while 61% did not.

Our team determined to look at our literacy practices as an attempt to answer the question: *What literacy practices prevail from third to sixth grades?* Here is a transcription of one of our principal research team's observations:

Date: 3/26/2020
Place: Pioneer View Elementary School Room 13
Participants: Second grade class and teacher
Observation focus: Reading Fluency
Starting time: 12:50
Ending time: 1:15
Observer: Muna Bishr

Participant	Observation	Codes	Groups	Category	Memo
Teacher	[Students are seated on the carpet in front of the teacher who is seated in a chair]. "Today we are going to learn about how we don't read too fast or too slow, we read just right and scoop the words together."				
Student	"If we read too slow we sound like robots."				
Teacher	"Readers, what is the strategy we learned so we read just right?"				
Student	"We scoop the words together!"				
Teacher	"Readers, do we do that with tricky words that we don't know?"				
A few students	"No!"				
Teacher	"No. What kind of words do we do that with?" [Teacher calls on student]. "Do you know what they are called? Do you remember?"				

Participant	Observation	Codes	Groups	Category	Memo
[Student shakes head].	"No."				
Teacher	"Let's help him out everybody. They're called . . .."				
All students:	"SNAP!'				
Teacher	"They are called 'snap' words because we know them in a . . .."				
All students	"SNAP!" [Students and teacher snap fingers].				
Teacher	"So, readers, instead of waiting until you find them talking like this [teacher talks like a robot], the first thing you are going to do is go back and see, 'Where are my snap words?' 'Where are my words that I can scoop up?' And when you put them together [pause] stop it now, you're going to stop it now [pause] and when you put them together [pause] you'll be able to read all the parts you colored." [After a brief pause teacher asks] "An old lady who swallowed a fly? And we have been practicing, look at me, look at me. What are words that I know in a snap, not just in this text but in others. You are going to color in all of your 'snap' words. Should I see this whole thing colored green?" [Everybody has a paper]				

Participant	Observation	Codes	Groups	Category	Memo
All students:	"No!"				
Teacher	"No. I am looking for words, not just in this story, but in any story. Got it? Off you go. [Students move from the carpet to their desks]. Okay, have a seat, get started." [Students take papers to their seats and use color pencils. They sit in groups of four, and have color pencils at their tables to choose from].				
Student	"Why do I have to get pink? I don't like pink."				
Teacher	"Remember, this is one that				
Teacher [talking to a student]	we really had to work on, so I don't want you to color this one because it's not a 'snap' for you. It's easy for you now because you know the story. I really want you to remember which ones did you know in a 'snap'? Like I, you can definitely color." [Teacher moves to front of room]. "I am going to count down from 5 and you are going to be looking for your 'snap' words. You are not talking to your neighbor: 4, 3, 2, 1. We are not talking to her right now because you have a really important job right now. You are not talking to me either. Look here, friends." [Teacher rings bell].				

Participant	Observation	Codes	Groups	Category	Memo
Teacher	"Full attention. Eyes up here. Eyes up here. Eyes up here. Every single person put your pencil down. Put it down. You're just looking over here. Look what, Alice [a student] did. Look what she did." [Teacher projects student's paper on smart board]. "Alice knows this whole story by heart right now. She can say it with her eyes closed. I can say it without even looking at it. Who can say it without even looking at it? I know right? Friends! Look at what she colored. She only colored words that she knows in a 'snap', no matter where they are. Not in a story she can sing. Not in a story she knows by heart. Look, I know, old, swallowed a fly, she, guy [talking to a student] you see how she starts scooping those words together because she knows that [sic] some of them without looking, not all of them, some of them no matter what story they are in; try to be like Alice. Really think about which words are a 'snap' for you no matter where they are."				
Student	"It's this right?"				

Participant	Observation	Codes	Groups	Category	Memo
Teacher	"Is it right for you? Are those words you know like this [teacher snaps fingers] that you know wherever you see them?" [Student nods].				
Teacher	"Then high five, right here. Keep going."				
Teacher [talks to a student]	"Okay, you are coloring every single word. You know why you are doing that? Because you know this story inside and out. What word is that? What word is this? See how you stopped for a second there? This is not a 'snap' word for you, but you can color this one. What word is that? See how you're stopping? That is not a 'snap' word for you. Okay? So, if you have to stop for a second, you don't color it. Even a second. Okay? Keep going. You're doing great. Keep going."				
Teacher [talking to different student]	"Look at each word and ask yourself, can you read it in a 'snap'? If not, don't color it."				
Teacher [talking to a group of students]	"Okay boys, how are you doing? Looks good. How are you deciding which one gets a color? Good. Excellent."				
Teacher [talking to another student in a different group]	"So here's how you are going to do it. Look at each word. What's that word? What word is it? Not the letter, the word. What word is it? Bum bada bum bum."				

Participant	Observation	Codes	Groups	Category	Memo
Students	"Bum, bum."				
Teacher	"Friends, as you finish coloring in your 'snap' words, Fran had a really good strategy. She looked at each word. If she had to look at it or think about it she said, nope, this isn't my 'snap' word. As you finish coloring your 'snap' words, you are going to turn and practice scooping them up with the person sitting next to you. Don't sing the song." [A student starts singing].				
Teacher	"You are not going to say it too fast [teacher says it really fast] and you are not going to say it too slow like a robot." [Teacher says it really slowly].				
Teacher	"How do you do that?" [Some students turn and start reading to partner. Some students finish coloring 'snap' words].				
Student	"I can count real fast . . .1, 2, 3, 4, 5,"				
Teacher	[Teacher rings bell]: "So, what I was expecting was for you to finish looking and then start practicing the reading part with the person sitting next to you."				

Participant	Observation	Codes	Groups	Category	Memo
Teacher	[Talking to student who took out a book.] "You'll try this one next, let's try this one first." [Teacher puts book back and puts paper in front of the student]. "Who is ready to practice with, S?"				
Student	"Me!"				
Teacher	"Okay, come over here with Sarah." [Student moves to sit next to Sarah].				
Teacher	"Who is ready to practice with, Alice?" [A student raises right hand].				
Teacher	"Come on over here. You are going to read to each other. Are you ready to start 'scooping'? Are you ready to read? Come read with, Hillary. Good. Keep going. Keep 'snapping.' 'Snapping' it up. Are you scooping? You are not looking at the words. You are remembering. I want you to read. Scoop 'em up."				
Teacher	[Talking to student] "Okay, start reading. Get your lips ready. Let's try again. What?"				
Student	"Ms. Brie, this is what I did." [student walks over to bulletin board and points to two reading strategies.] "Chunky Monkey!"				

Participant	Observation	Codes	Groups	Category	Memo
Teacher	"That's right, I heard you go mmmm to sound out the word. If you are done, pull out a book to read. Sit down, please."				

Resources

Gather
https://gathercapture.com/
Survey monkey
https://www.surveymonkey.com
Fulcrum
https://info.fulcrumapp.com/
Indeemo
https://indeemo.com/
Christine D. Clayton, & James F. Kilbane (2020). *Inquiry in Tandem.* New York: Peter Lang.

6 | The Analysis

> It happens like an aha! And then another aha! A series of aha's. Truth emerges as little explosions, one after the other. Amazing surprises.
>
> Sunday García (interview, 1/15, 2020)

Nowadays we can analyze great amounts of qualitative data fairly fast and effectively. Digital technology makes it possible for us to input considerable amounts of qualitative data and execute whatever analysis we need. Yet, while the speed of analysis has dramatically increased, discovery still triggers great surprises and professional satisfaction. These are powerful whether we find these new truths through digital means, or manually. These applications, nonetheless, signify a great advance to the field. Nowadays, we simply need to do a search, such as "digital qualitative data analysis applications," and surely enough we will see on our screen a whole list of applications. Check them out and select the one that meets your needs.

Similar to understanding the concept of multiplication before using a calculator, for the purposes of this book we want to present the fundamentals of qualitative data analysis that most algorithms have followed. Once we have a good grasp of the grounding ideas and procedures, and depending on the extent of the study, one may choose to conduct the analysis manually or digitally.

Let's start with four vital notions.

- *First,* qualitative data means text, that is, the written word. We can easily transfer sound data—from recordings—to written text. We can also transfer visuals, albeit more expensively, from film, or video into text. In any case, the principle here is that to conduct good, rigorous qualitative data analysis, we are better off if data are in a written text format. This includes archival documentation. Photographs, charts, and other visuals that cannot be narrated in written form, may actually serve as illustrations that speak in a summarized form, as the saying goes "a picture is worth a thousand words."
- *Second,* keep in mind that data analysis does not have to wait for all data to be collected. While it is a distinctive step after data collection, we do analyze the evidence along the way. The principle here is that data collection and data analysis run as a parallel process. Yet, we privilege data collection when doing so; the moment we sit down to decipher data's content and unearth from there complex meanings, we also dedicate our full attention to doing so. Moreover, similar to our openness to do analysis while collecting data, we do keep a watchful eye on emerging new data collection needs when analyzing data.
- *Third,* data analysis implies discovery, whenever the reality under scrutiny speaks to us. The collected evidence, therefore, reveals its meanings to us, not the other way around—namely, we do not tell what reality is, but data do. We need to be ready for surprises; unexpected results may push our study in unexpected directions, catapult it in a promising trajectory, or reversing all efforts back to the planning stage. Our analytic job encompasses the act of generating understanding from the ground up. This inferential approach sits at the center of collaborative action research applied to data analysis. Thus, at the stage of analysis we do not judge, conclude, or propose solutions.
- *Fourth,* analysis can only be done when and if we create data boundaries. Gathering data may become addictive, thus fixing clear starting and ending points is of crucial importance. Once we know where to start and where to end collecting data, it is possible to not only avoid the overwhelming sense that large amounts of qualitative data might provoke, but also to realize that analysis is attainable. When gathering longitudinal data,

determining a starting date point and an ending date point may save us time, money, and other resources.

Summing up: qualitative data equal text; organizing and analyzing may run simultaneously; reality leads data collection; start and end data collection and data analysis at precise points and dates.

Qualitative data analysis consists first of data reduction, and second, data display. In the following sections, we explain how data reduction works, how to display data, and then how to prepare a report.

Data Reduction

Managing large amounts of pages of written text often presents a daunting task to the principal research team. The first task then consists of breaking the data into usable chunks, then cutting the chunks into slices as thin as possible, and after that, coding the slices. Think of this process as equivalent to our attempt to eat a baguette. This long and narrow French bread is of not much use if we do not cut it into smaller pieces. We do the same with data. Once we have finished coding, we look for patterns and group them all. The final step is creating large categories from these groups (see Figure 6.1).

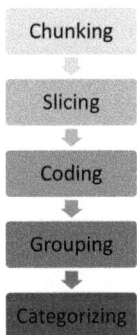

Figure 6.1: Data reduction steps
Source: G. Arriaza © 2020

Chunking

Chunking up data is carried out by marking data based on meaningful indicators. One way to do this is by identifying where an event starts and where it ends. The above sample from researcher Melissa Reese shows us already a good chunk. The goal of the observation was "whole class language arts" in Mrs. Bee's 2nd grade classroom. As a stand-alone, these data are a snippet of the classroom dynamics. In other words, the data show us the researcher capturing the delivery of a language arts lesson, as a part, a chunk, of a series of other observations, earlier that day. The oral communication starts:

Our next word is 'defeat'. What is defeat?

The use of "next" suggests that there were other words, and other activities before the researcher started the observation.

A chunk, as a piece of baguette, belongs to a larger unit. Our example covers 38 minutes of an observation of two hours. The chunk is one event—the teaching of vocabulary. The teaching of vocabulary is delivered first through the intentional use of some words (defeat, worry, code, and eager), and then by directed text reading of a story (one that contains "beginning, middle, and end" as Mrs. Bee tells).

The details the researcher provides within brackets help us to understand the context of the event, and to capture non-verbal communication.

The researcher opens the event by describing where and how teacher and students stood: [*Teacher is sitting at a chair while students are sitting crisscross at the carpet in no particular order. Teacher is holding up a card with a word and a picture on it*].

The actual event starts with: "*Our next word is 'defeat,'*" and finishes with the teacher saying: "*OK, leave this where it is. Let's go to lunch.*"

The observer closes the event with this description: [*Teacher and students start to walk out the door. Soft student chatter takes place as they exit*].

Bracketed descriptions play a crucial role by supplying information of the social and physical surroundings of verbal exchanges, as well as gestures and other body communication. The latter add a very important communication dimension to the spoken word; these details enhance our comprehension and further the analysis.

The second step after we chunk the data is cutting the chunk up into smaller parts.

Slicing

Having bounded our data (chunking), we now need to reduce each chunk into smaller, workable pieces. We are ready to cut it, following our baguette analogy, into slices. In Melissa Reese's sample, we distinguish two slices.

Slice one—refers to the use of concrete vocabulary words.

It starts with "*Our next word is 'defeat,' What is defeat?*" and it ends with "*Right, if you're eager you're very excited or interested. Those are our vocab words for this week. O.k. we are going to go back to our desks and get out Benchmark.*"

Slice two refers to reading comprehension.

It starts with the closing statement of slice one. In the third sentence the teacher asks students: [. . .] *O.k. we are going to go back to our desks and get out Benchmark*, which is followed by this description: [*Teacher and students walk back to desks. Quiet talking is taking place amongst students.*]

Physical action tails the teacher's words, which elicits a clear distinction between the end of a slice (or activity) and the beginning of another. These slices can be further thin sliced into smaller ones. We can examine, the specific activity with each word of the vocabulary, and also do the same with the text reading that follows. In our example, we can thin slice the first section of the text into: defeat, worry, code, and eager.

Coding

Now that we have chunked data from researcher Reed's study (one observation) sliced it (two slices), and thin-sliced one of these, we are prepared to dig some more, in search of deeper meanings. We need to do this work orderly and purposefully. Coding means that we index the text wherever we uncover something of importance to the research question and study purposes.

Coding is also a new step in the process of reducing our data to significant—in terms of meaning and size—pieces. Prior to subjecting the data to this process, we recommend the creation of a code key. Keeping in mind that this sense-making effort must stay tightly linked to the research question and within the parameters of the study's purpose, we build the code key considering three points: codes most be easy to retrieve, must be explicit in terms of what they mean, and short (one word, or a phrase). Moreover, we use this code key as guideline, and not as a mandate. Not only we do not have to use all codes we invent a priori, but must be open-minded enough to allow data determine which codes ultimately fit.

Following researcher Reed's study sample, we know that we want to build our code key around these points: (a) Better understanding of the different literacy methods; and (b) address the question—How do lower elementary school children decipher reading content? (see Table 6.1).

Table 6.1: Code-Key

Code	Meaning
Vocabuild	Vocabulary building as a purposeful effort to learn new words.
Worduse	The application of new words in new sentences.
Directeach	Teaching by telling.
Expmean	Explaining meaning in abstract.
Recallfacts	Remember individualized facts.
Storyseq	Story sequence from book stories with beginning, middle, and end.
Socont	Social control, external attribution discipline.
Rightontxt	Right on the text facts finding.
Posienforce	Positive enforcement of in class behavior

Source; G. Arriaza © 2020

We may add a prefix to each of these codes so that to mark them clearly, for instance we can add date, case number, observer ID. So, code "vocab build" could read: 20190100vacabild (year 2019, case 01, researcher 00).

Conducting data analysis triggers a multiplicity of reactions. The moment we determine the significance of a piece of data and apply a code, we are rationally marking the text based on what we believe it means, in relation to the study's question and purpose. At any moment, while doing this work, a piece of data may trigger thoughts and feelings tied to or independent from the study's question and purpose. As we have previously stated, capturing these momentary thoughts and feelings as memos to yourself is a key research habit. See template Table 6.2 below.

Table 6.2: Coding Template

Text	Code	Memo

Source: G. Arriaza @ 2020

Here is the first coded slice:

Text	Code	Memo
[Teacher is sitting at a chair while students are sitting criss-cross at the carpet in no particular order. Teacher is holding up a card with a word and a picture on it].		Word with no context. General definitions Applies behavioral norms on the spot
"Our next word is 'defeat.' What is defeat?" [Nods at student raising his hand].	Vocabuild	
"For example, U.S. won against Belgium so U.S. defeated Belgium." [Another male student starts speaking]	Worduse	
"I defeated them. It means you lose."		
"I like it. Alright, defeat means to win a victory over someone in a battle or contest" [Teacher stops and quietly talks to a student] "Are you chewing gum? I hope you're not chewing gum. We already went over this. Whatever is [sic] in your mouth, please throw it away."	Worduse Expmean Directeach	
[Student gets up and walks quietly to the trash can to throw something away. Some students turn to look, but the teacher is moving quickly on with the lesson].		
"Another vocabulary word this week is 'worry.' What does that mean?" [Makes eye contact to acknowledge female student raising her hand]	Vocabuild	
"'Worry' is like when you get lost. You get sad."		
[Student speaks without being called on], "My mom always worries."	Worduse Worduse	
"Good. Worry means to feel uneasy or uncertain about what will happen. Our next word is 'code.'"	Expmean Vocabuild	
"Ummm … something in a box, you need a code."	Directeach	
"Oh, right. Like with our chrome book cart. We put in a code to open it and get the chrome books. This kind of code means there is a set of laws or rules about how to behave. That's what this kind of code means. Code is a multiple meaning word."	Worduse Expmean Directeach	
[Speaks without being called on], "like my video game, I need to put in a code to unlock the next level."	Worduse	
[Teacher moves on without acknowledging student's statement]. "Our last word is 'eager.'"	Vocabuild	
"Like happy to do something."		
"Curious"	Worduse	
"Excited"	Worduse	
"Right, if you're eager you're very excited or interested. Those are our vocab words for this week […]"	Worduse Expmean Directeach	

The Analysis | 171

Grouping

After we have exhausted coding our data, we need to look for patterns. Typically, we group codes from the easiest to the most difficult patterns. The first codes to bring together are the identical ones. The second codes are those related, as in a family tree. The third codes to get together are those that fall within a field. After all these reduction process, we may still end up with a few impossible to group codes. We treat these as standing alone codes. We may want to organize them as outliers, and eventually into a category called "unexpected results."

Identical Codes: These codes refer to the same topic and labeled identically. In our small sample above we have a repeat of four codes, which now become "groups":

> worduse (eight times)
> vocabuild (four times)
> expmean (four times)
> directeach (four times)

In other words, we have reduced the entire slice to four codes.

Before we move on to the next step, let's keep in mind this point: data are flagged through codes. Therefore, we need to trace each code to its source. Having this tracking established allows us to come back, any time we need to, to the data that originated the code.

Creating a contact sheet matrix is a great aid for data tracking. The matrix contains: code, content, page, exact line. See Table 6.3

Table 6.3: Data Tracking Contact Sheet

Code	Verbatim Text	Page	Line

We coded the second data slice separately, and collapsed all those that were identical. Here is the list:

Family Codes: To further reduce our data, we look for those identical codes that may have a close topical relationship, as members of the same trunk. In our example, we so far have four identical codes from the first data slice, and five from the second for a total of nine:

> Worduse
> Vocabuild

Expmean
Directeach
Recallfacts
Storyseq
Socont
Right on txt
Posienforce

Now we can group the codes "worduse," "vocabbuild," and "expmean" as a family set referring to a topic we call "*lexicon building.*"

We can also group the codes "recallfacts," "storyseq," and "right on txt" as a family set referring to the topic "*reading strategies.*"

We can group the codes "soccont," and "posienforce" as a family set referring to the topic "*discipline.*"

However, the code "*directeach,*" does not fit into any of the families created. Perhaps this code may join other codes the rest of the data (all the classroom observations and the interviews) may produce. For now, we will keep it as outlier, and, if our data do not change, it may become one we may treat as unexpected finding.

So far, we have created three groups: lexicon building, reading strategies, discipline, and have a left alone the code "directeach."

Categorizing

We have now three groups:

Lexicon building
Reading strategies
Discipline

And one lonly code:
Directeach

From these groups we just created, we now can start building larger ones. We need to collapse those groups based on topic proximity to a field. This means that at this point we are ready to create larger, more abstract groups.

For instance, "lexicon building" and "reading strategies" may be grouped together under the field "literacy." Discipline, on the other hand, does not. Data reduction has left us with two categories: Literacy, and Discipline.

We still carry one single code: Directeach.

Themes

Large-scale studies generate equally large number of categories. Our work then consists of identifying patterns among categories and bringing together those that can be collapsed into a theme, so that at the end of our analysis we wind up with a manageable number of themes. Collapsing categories into themes follows the same criteria we have applied so far: (a) join categories that belong to the same topical family; (b) collapse categories that share a topical proximity into fields, and (c) leave alone, but do not ignore, categories that do not fit together.

Tracking Reduction

Keep close track of the reduction process. Create a map showing a destination list of codes, groups, categories, and themes. This way you know exactly which codes became groups, which groups became a category, and which categories became a theme, and so on (see Table 6.4).

Table 6.4: Reduction Map

Code	Groups	Category	Theme	Meta-theme
Word use	Lexicon building	Literacy		
Vocab build	Lexicon building	Literacy		
Exp mean	Lexicon building	Literacy	Literacy	
Directeach	?	?	?	
Recall facts	Reading strategies	Literacy		
Storyseq	Reading strategies	Literacy		
Socont	Discipline	Discipline	Discipline	
Right on txt	Reading strategies	Literacy		
Posienforce	Discipline	Discipline		

Source: G. Arriaza © 2020

In sum, data reduction follows a systematic and logical process that operates from the ground level up from the evidence collected as written text, to ever more abstract constructs—from codes, to groups, to categories to themes. If at the end of the creation of themes we still haven't found a larger construct for the categories we identified through the analysis of patterns, we must decide whether to include them in a section labeled "unexpected results," or leave them aside for later study. We repeat: In the same way that outliers in numerical data, we do not ignore the codes, groups, or categories lacking a pattern (see Figure 6.2).

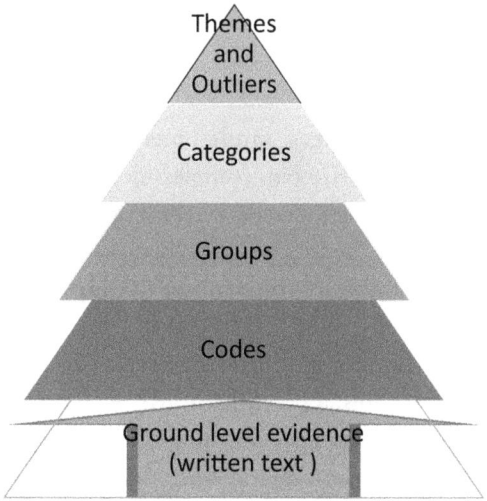

Figure 6.2: Code Key
Source: G. Arriaza © 2020

Data Display

After we have exhausted our data analysis, we should be ready to move on to the next step—data display. The systematic use of the *data tracking contact sheet* (see Table 6.6) should make the task of retrieving verbatim data quite feasible.

Selecting and deciding how to present data entails a decision governed by the answers found to our research question, the purposes of the study, and the audience the study purports to serve. Qualitative data must coherently speak to the findings. Thus, qualitative data display consists of the appropriate use of data to support each and every claim the study makes. Substantiating every claim also contributes to address the study's rigor, and to showcase the robust nature of the evidence collected. Data display offers the opportunity to make explicit what has been omitted, placed on the margins, or ignored. This is particularly true of accounts of social groups pushed out of the formalized, official narrative. In the history of social sciences, we find an extensive tradition of first-person sociological studies, as well as testimony and counter-narratives in the realm of cultural studies.

In a study report, data are displayed in the findings and the discussion of findings sections. The layout of these sections typically follows one of these structures: (1) organize findings around the research questions, or (2) organize findings around the themes unearthed through the analysis.

Inspiring Quotations

Data often yields statements, images, similes, metaphors, and symbols that capture deep thoughts and summarize big, complex ideas. Take note of these bits of data when memoing, annotating journals, or reading the data contact sheet. You may want to display them at the foot of titles. Instead of searching for inspiring brief text somewhere else, cultivate the habit of finding them within your own data sets.

Examples: 1. In a study lead by Elizabeth Brook Garza on dual immersion education in elementary schools, a participant, Ms. A. Reyes, expressed her position about students' home language. She summarized a whole series of ideas about language ownership, respect, and identity this way:

> **I make a big deal about how they're the experts. This is their**
>
> **language. They are the knowledgeable people**
>
> (A. Reyes, personal communication)

2. In an interview conducted by one of us, Gilberto, on the potential application of critical language awareness to daily social interactions, one of the participants synthesized the entirety of this approach's meaning and purpose, this way:

> **Critical language awareness is about**
>
> **dismantling injustice one word at a time**
>
> (M. Jones, interview series)

Supportive Statements

Display short statements (one to two sentences) within an argument to provide support, clarity, or emphasis to the argument's point. In addition, weaving within the narrative of a study's findings the participants' language aids the narrative to bridging its technical reporting to real-life situations.

Examples: 1. In her study about African American and Latinx students access to STEM careers, researcher Yvonne L. White inserts the voice of one of her study participants as an emphasis to the issue of harsh disciplinary actions the author is exposing:

> Mr. Aye asserts that punishing students for offenses arising from issues that they have no control over is punishing them twice. In his experience as a principal he has many stories. Stories about having worked with parents, teachers and students themselves in behavior modification programs to manage some of these realities. "I am not saying that this is easy by any means, What I am saying, is that it is doable if we find it in our hearts." (J. Aye. Interviews) Mr. Aye remarks with a compassionate face.

2. In her study about dual immersion, Elizabeth Brook Garza inserts her participants' description of intentional teaching:

> Isabel also stated that she gives power to the native Spanish-speakers, by "highlighting their worth and their intelligence and really encouraging" (I. Cruz. Interviews). During group work she assigns the Spanish-speakers to leadership roles. Isabel commented, "They are the experts. Demonstrating that, modeling, that every group has a Spanish-speaker, and they're the expert, they're the leader of that group." (I. Cruz. Interviews)

Evidentiary Material

Display full paragraphs, or paragraph sections from the data as the evidence itself, or as long illustration of the issue being presented.
Example: 1. Researcher Yvonne L. White, from above, shows how participants understand classroom activities and their connection to real world labor:

This may be of particular benefit to minoritized students who do not see themselves, their values, or their culture expressed in traditional classroom curriculum. Furthermore, Lee stated:

So seeing somebody else at work, doing what they're doing in the classroom, and mak[ing] money out of it is very revealing to a lot of these students. I've been in a lot of situations where I see the students [say] 'Oh yeah, we did that last week.' And this guy's doing it and, you know, the light bulb goes on in their head. And I think that in itself — work-based learning, in itself, provides that guidance to students, so they're not just learning things in a theoretical way. (T. Lee, interview)

As Lee suggests, experiential learning opportunities make the connection between classroom curriculum, work skills, and future income opportunities.
2. Researcher Elizabeth Brook Garza, from above, illustrates the utter fragility of dual immersion programs, due in part to the disproportionate influence of the families of English native speakers.

In order to attain the 50/50 language ratio, the teachers in the program make great efforts to attract and keep more English-speaking families. They may accommodate the English-speaking students more so as not to have them leave the program. Elsa related:

Whereas the other ones [the native English-speaking students] you're like, "OK, let's tip-toe around this." Maybe their behavior is horrible, but some teachers might turn an eye. Whereas the other ones [the native Spanish-speaking students] you are right on top of them. I'm just talking in generalities, what I've seen in our program.

It's like the eggshell parents, and then the ones who are bare bones. This is how it is, and I hate to say that. That's what I see trending, and we try to avoid that. Because you don't want them to feel like, "Well, they get away with this," because you want to keep them in the program, because they're the parents who are like, "Well, we're leaving." You want to hold on to them, and it's horrible, because that might change how teachers are treating some of the kids. You always try and keep them. Then you also get frustrated (E. Gray, personal communications).

Vignettes

Display short illustrative stories as examples, as synthesis of a study's finding, or also as conduits for an entire argument. Typically, vignettes are placed at the head of a publication, or immediately after a finding, or a discussion of a finding has been argued. They serve as a device that forewarns the reader of the actual details of said finding or argument, or illustrates the entire argument. Throughout this book we have used them as introductory points. In Chapter One, for instance, we bring a first-person account of an incident that raises key issues around agency and agents of change.

A vignette is built directly from a story depicting an action, a series of events, individuals, or group(s) activities.

Sample: A teacher tells a story about dual language learners at her site. The story depicts the low academic tracking of these children, and along with it, the potential for lowering the professional status of teachers working with this population. The vignette captures a central social justice concern of a study, conducted by Gilberto, on this topic. The label "language exclamation" refers to a lockstep, highly scripted, literacy program adapted as solution to the learning of English language by US born or immigrant Latinx children in middle school.

> I'm teaching three periods of language exclamation to all Latino children. They're all from impoverished homes. This program consists of second grade skills. These children stay together. After my class they travel together to a math, science and one elective. We call them language exclamation kids. All first generation US born. They had English instruction since second grade and yet they're at this reading level. They were promoted to sixth grade and that's the question. Why? These kids may have some learning disability as well. But we don't test them and do not provide special education services to them.

> They all know they're behind. They know who's strong and who is weak. We tell them the truth. And help them with self-esteem. We've had lots of discussion about their academic grades. I, for one, do not want to give "As" because that's misleading. Parents wouldn't ask their kids to do their work if they're getting "As". Then also the SAT scores come from the state showing how low they are, and parents will complain, "what are you telling us?", they may ask.

> Teachers don't want to be told what to teach and in language exclamation it is totally scripted. So teachers being asked to teach this program, adamantly oppose to do so. In my experience I don't think there's a prestige (low or high)

associated to the subject matter we teach. In my experience I've never heard or saw a higher reputation to me because of this teaching.

Profiles

Displaying sketches or full narratives showing the actual life, personality, behaviors, or traditions and habits of people and institutions, may serve as a way to bring to the forefront participant's opinions, worldviews. Profiling allows participants to speak in the first person, thus inviting readers to close the distance—cultural, social, and otherwise—with the narrator. In other words, profiling weaves narratives that otherwise may never be heard, which may even counter dominant ones.

Example: Researcher Brook Garza profiles one individual. The researcher tells how the mother tongue plays front and central as source of affirmation and pride for the profiled individual, a bilingual speaker, in a society where, even today, the exclusivity of monolingualism functions as a defining factor. The author weaves her analysis along with the story being told by Isabel Cruz, a participant, this way:

> I describe the teachers' personal experiences; this encompasses the teacher's ethnicity, language background, schooling experiences, training, and teaching history. I also reveal the participants' own descriptions of their class and community demographics and background.

Isabel Cruz

Isabel teaches fifth grade dual immersion at Creekside Elementary in Ridgeline, an affluent suburban city. She describes herself as "Cuban, Hispanic." Spanish was her first language but she learned English before she entered school. For Isabel her heritage and ability to speak Spanish was a source of pride. She states, "So, I think that I probably spoke English at two, three years of age. People admired me that I spoke Spanish. It was always a real positive thing for me." She sees her students display shame or embarrassment to speak it, and adds, "I was never embarrassed. I didn't feel different. Sometimes in Ridgeline that's a little different [. . .]." She feels that two-way immersion is part of the 'work' to counter the negativity associated with Spanish and Latino background. Indeed, as Isabel states, Spanish has been a positive asset that has opened opportunities for her. Her students see it differently. Isabel states

> For me, I don't see Spanish as that low socioeconomic status. I don't feel that way. It's landed me this job, for crying out loud. It's been a huge part of my life since I was small. I didn't have these experiences growing up...Sometimes these

kids are a little embarrassed to speak Spanish or just want to speak in English. They want to blend in and they want to fit in, and that wasn't my experience. It was always like my life. This is what made me different. There's work to be done in Ridgeline. I don't know if I'm allowed to say that where we are, but there's work to be done (I. Cruz, personal communication, February 1, 2012).

She has been teaching for 11 years, nine of those years in two-way immersion. She states her reason for first teaching two-way immersion this way: "It was sort of the credential that I had and my background and the job openings. I sort of just fell into it. It wasn't something that I sought out." She states that the difficulty of the job surprised her, she is amazed by the high standards the program demands of the students in both languages and feels much pressure to push the students to maintain those high levels of proficiency in both languages. Isabel describes the challenges and pressure in the following terms:

It's the most challenging assignment ever known on the face of this Earth. I could be a CEO at this point. [laughs] It is the most challenging job. It surprises me that we really expect these kids to perform like native speakers at this stage of the game. The resources that we have to do that[. . .] A lot of parents do work with their children at home and encourage Spanish, and then you have a lot of people who do not. That's a huge eye-opening thing for me, how it's so much pressure. It's so much what we're expected to do.

She is excited to see her students reaching high levels. She asserts: "But it also surprised me how amazing it is and how much these kids are learning despite all of those things, and how amazing they're doing and how they are learning, and that's super cool." Despite the difficulties she wants to continue teaching in two-way immersion. She has a strong sense of commitment to the program and has enrolled her son in the Creekside Dual Immersion program. Isabel says, "I totally own this program. I put my own son in this program."

Although she has a strong sense of belief and commitment, Isabel also has concerns. In her fifth-grade class of 27 students, only five students are native Spanish speakers. She sees a discrepancy between the status of her native Spanish speakers and native English-speakers. She would like to make the program more equitable and wonders if the Ridgeline school district two-way program is meeting all its goals. Isabel feels that the program is doing a satisfactory job with the bilingualism and biliteracy aims of the two-way program. "As far as bilingualism and biliteracy goes, I think that yes, we're doing a really fair job."

However, she does not see the biculturalism component of the program taking hold. Isabel states that the cross-cultural component of the Creekside Dual Immersion program is stuck at superficial levels that focus on the "light and fluffy." This concerns her. She notes:

> I struggle with this one. I think that it might be a Creekside problem in particular, or in Ridgeline. I'm not sure, but I don't think that biculturalism is happening at all. I think that we celebrate some holidays and we do some really light, fluffy stuff, but I don't know if kids really get a sense of another culture and appreciate that. I don't think that we're doing a really good job with that. What I see in fifth grade, I get discouraged sometimes.

Nevertheless, Isabel feels that for the most part, both groups of students are better off participating in the two-way program. At the end of fifth grade the students are, as she puts it—"not finished," and they still have years to continue their growth. She is unsure, but feels that dual immersion has laid a valuable foundation of confidence for the Spanish speakers. Both groups will benefit from the opportunities their background in dual immersion will open for them. She feels both groups are better off participating in dual immersion. Isabel comments:

> That's positive because it might lead to open up doors for them in the future. It gives those Spanish speakers that confidence That confidence helps you. It goes to other areas. That it is valuable, for both parties. They're better off. Dual immersion is definitely the right program for these kids, and it can only be a benefit. I don't think that they're worse off [. . .] I do see a sense of pride in the dual immersion students.

Composites

Depicting a composite profile helps a researcher to capture large numbers of individuals or organizations in an abbreviated format. It can contain a combination of commonly shared traits and characteristics from several individuals or institutions. For instance, a group of individuals may share defining features such as—same institutional affiliation, racial and ethnic identification, level of formal education, bilingualism, and first-generation immigration experience. A set of institutions may share features and traits such as same geographical area, similar demographics of staff, type of service, and clientele base.

Composites stitch together those core common defining features, traits, and characteristics into one collective story that mirrors all the individual stories. To create this common story, this organizer may help:

Table 6.5: Composite Matrix

Participants	Affiliation	Self-Described Racial/Ethnic Group	Gender	Degree Formal Education	Salient Lived Experiences With (Define the One Aspect from Collected Data)

Source G. Arriaza © 2020

Once salient features have been indexed the writing of the story must:

(a) Compile the commonalities from the data collected in the composite index;
(b) Tabulate the features that can be measured (e.g., constructs such as gender, income, and age);
(c) Write the narrative combining all features or attributes commonly shared (systematized in "a" and "b"), highlight the ones not commonly shared, and insert any firsthand accounts from the participants' data to illustrate the composite profile.

Quantifying Words

Using digital technology assists us translating words into numbers, compute some statistics, and produce graphs. Digital applications can easily do this work with large amounts of data. Typically, these programs can run for us, for instance, a frequency analysis. We enter the words we need to tabulate, and the application will produce the frequency and actual context of use. For example, let's take the 975 words of the above individual profile, Isabel Cruz. We could do an analysis of words, such as "shame," "embarrassment," "status," "better off," "pride," and find out when these were used and whether the attribution belongs to the author, researcher Brook Garza, or the participant, Isabel Cruz. See template below.

Table 6.6: Frequency Analysis

Word	Frequency	Context
Shame	1 author	She sees her students display shame or embarrassment to speak it
Embarrassment	1 author 3 Ms. Cruz	She sees her students display shame or embarrassment to speak it, "I was never embarrassed. I didn't feel different." "Sometimes these kids are a little embarrassed to speak Spanish or just want to speak in English." "I was never embarrassed. I didn't feel different."
Status	2	
Better Off	2 author 1 Ms. Cruz	Isabel feels that for the most part, both groups of students are better off participating in the two-way program She feels both groups are better off participating in dual immersion "They're better off. Dual immersion is definitely the right program for these kids"
Pride	1 author 1 Ms. Cruz	Spanish was a source of pride. "I do see a sense of pride in the dual immersion students"

Source: G. Arriaza © 2020

Now we have, just from this small data sample, a good sense of the importance of primary language attachment to both the author, and the participant. The tabulated data serve as proof of a discussion on the role, for instance, primordial attachments play in one's connections to place and language.

Bringing It All Together: Reporting Findings

After we have finished first reducing, and second analyzing the evidence, we are ready to report the study results. Two of the most useful ways of reporting are: (1) organizing findings around the research question, and (2) organizing findings around the emerging themes. Additionally, given our intent to influence decision-making processes the most effective way of presenting our study report is by providing a summary.

Organizing Findings around the Research Question

Reporting results around the research question implies responding each of the ground-level, operative questions. In this case, we substantiate our answers to these questions with the themes we created. An outline of our report would look like this:

Introduction
Remind readers the challenge, purpose, and significance of the study. State the research question the study sought to respond.

First ground-level question
Provide the evidence supporting the claim by systematically referencing the data contained in the uncovered themes.

Second ground-level question
Provide the evidence supporting the claim by systematically referencing the data contained in the uncovered themes.

Keep listing the questions and their respective responses.

Summary of findings
Write a succinct narrative to stress the relevance of each finding.

Organizing Findings around Themes

In this case, the entire reporting of results follows each of the themes uncovered through the analysis. We weave the response to the questions by linking each theme to each of them. An outline of our report would look like this:

Findings

Introduction
Remind readers the challenge, purpose, and significance of the study. State the research question the study sought to respond.

First theme
Provide the evidence supporting the claim, and link it to first ground-level question.

Second theme
Provide the evidence supporting the claim, and link it to second ground-level question.

Keep listing the themes, link each to the ground-level question to which they respond.

Summary of findings

Bring all findings together in a succinct narrative to stress the relevance of each finding.

Executive Summary

A full study report takes significant amounts of pages. Not all members of our targeted audience will necessarily read the entirety of a report. Since collaborative action research's core purpose is to provide new understandings on challenges affecting our organization, and thus enact revolutionary changes, we must provide our study results in readable formats. At the head of our report we always provide a summary in the form of an executive summary. We assume that this compacted way of presenting large reports will secure its reading by those individuals who need to pay attention to our work.

We assume that most leaders and policy makers do not necessarily have the time for reading whole study reports. Yet, we still need to inform their decision-making process. Here is the layout we have developed over years of practice:

1. *Start* with title of the study, authors' names, and date. Then write an *abstract:* 60–100 words (keep it short, and to the point). An abstract should capture the challenge, purpose of the study, core finding, and main recommendation.
2. *Definition of the challenge*: one full, short paragraph describing the challenge and its manifestations.
3. *Synthesis of core literature* references: Cite the most notable empirical and theoretical studies on the challenge's and action's core content. Do not exceed two paragraphs.
4. *Theory followed:* Write one paragraph explaining the central theoretical frame applied to the interpretation of the study's data.
5. *Key components of the methodology* approach: Name, in one to two paragraphs, the methodological approach and describe the key procedures followed.
6. *Central findings:* Carefully select the most salient findings and state them in no more than two paragraphs. List them in order of relevance.
7. *Most important interpretation (conclusions) and recommendation*: Write two to three paragraphs stating the interpretation of the main finding(s) and the ramifications in terms of policy, decision-making, organizational structures, budget, curriculum and instruction, or any other applied areas.

Sample:

Executive Summary

Context: Douglas Valley High School (DVHS) is the largest high school in the Raymond Unified School District, with approximately 3,400 students. It is the #4 ranked public school in the region and a National Blue Ribbon School qualifier. Within this population, 2.4% are English learners, 7.8% are considered socioeconomically disadvantaged, 5.2% are characterized as special education, and 0% of students are designated as foster youth. The school has a 97.8% graduation rate, a 95% attendance rate, and 88.7% of students are prepared for college. Overall, DVHS students score above the average national Advanced Placement scores and, since its implementation in 2014, have the highest district student performance and progress scores.

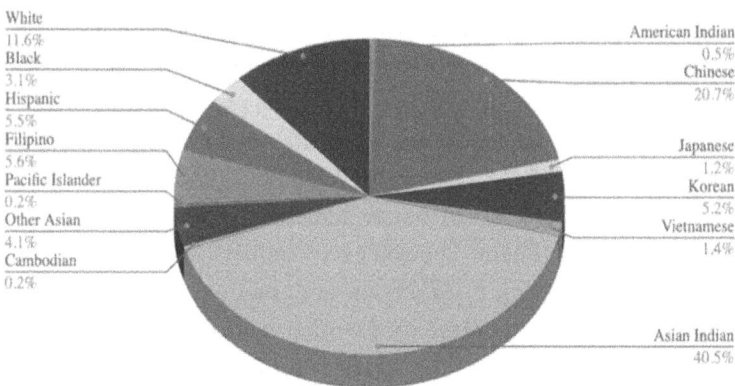

Challenge: There is an inverse relationship between student achievement and academic pressure and social and emotional health. At Douglas Valley High School, while students' overall academic performance and test scores are high, their social-emotional health is dangerously unstable, including reporting high levels of chronic sadness, anxiety, and suicidal ideation.

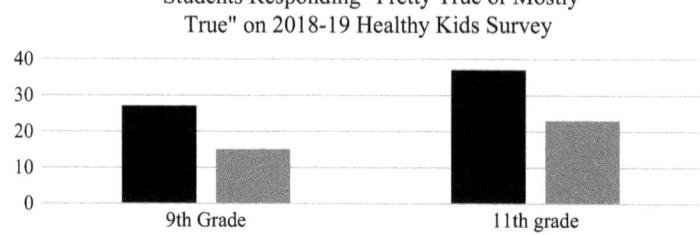

Literature Review: The Center for Disease Control reports alarming data regarding adolescent mental health, such as that 13–20% of youth experience serious mental health issues, including suicide, which is the third leading cause of death for 15–24-year-olds (Caldarella, Millet, Heath, Warren & Williams, 2019, p.3, as cited in CDC, 2013; Ward & Odegard, 2011, as cited in CDC, 2006). Students specifically taking advanced classes reported statistically significant higher overall perceived stress than general education students, citing various sources of stressors: the "perception of extreme pressure to achieve," parents, teachers, the general school community, and their management of commitments (Shaunessy-Dedrick, Suldo, & Roth, 2015, p. 112, 125). In dangerous combination with these rising levels of stress, adolescents either have far less developed coping mechanisms and control over conflicts and stressors (Matheny, Aycock, & McCarthy, 1993, p.112), often use emotion-focused coping, as they perceive events out of their control, or use other inadequate coping mechanisms (Wrzesniewsk & Chylinkska, 2007), often causing more struggles with mental health.

Question: What coping mechanisms are students using to respond to high academic stress?

Methodology: This is a hybrid convergence-sequential mixed-methods study of students' social emotional health, stress, anxiety, and coping mechanisms, which by definition "incorporates both qualitative and quantitative methods of data collection and analysis in a single study," where quantitative data drove the qualitative data (Creswell, 2007, p. 455). The study uses quantitative survey data from the unit of analysis, as well ethnographic-based qualitative data of interviews and field observations from a smaller subset.

The purpose of this study was to examine what coping mechanisms students are using to respond to such high academic pressure and achievement, with intended goals to deepen an understanding of how to best help students and find tangible action items to decrease their suicidal ideation and increase emotional stability and health.

Findings: Most students regard stress negatively, associating it with emotions like anxiety, fear, pressure, pain, sadness or feeling overwhelmed, as well as finding it consuming and fixed. Stress comes from many sources, but most frequently comes from school, family, and relationships.

Irrespective of gender, ethnicity, or age, most students self-identify as being task-oriented copers, but regarding stress specifically, students report using emotion and avoidance-based coping mechanisms. All students reported feeling high levels of anxiety, especially as a coping response. As grade level increases, so does the frequency of utilizing task-coping mechanisms.

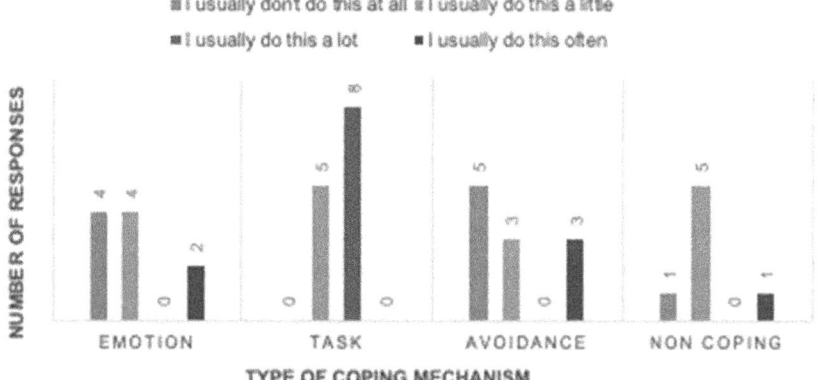

Regardless of gender, ethnicity, or age, students report high levels of self-efficacy, though feel more confident in their abilities to work out problems and try things than they do about "things they do well."

Overall, students feel connected to school, but miss school frequently, mostly due to physical illness, feeling unprepared or behind in school, not getting enough sleep and feeling stressed, sad, or angry.

Almost half of students report feeling chronically sad and almost a quarter seriously contemplated suicide, though the highest percentage of subgroups reporting this were 10th grade, female, and South Asian students.

190 | *Community-Owned Knowledge*

Discussion & Recommendation: These findings suggest that students are less "learning-oriented," focusing on learning and internalizing achievement, but more so "performance-oriented," desiring external, positive acknowledgement and perception of high ability (Brdar, Rijavec, Loncaric, 2006, p. 54, as cited in Meece, Blumenfeld, & Hoyle, 1988; Nicholls, 1989; Dweck, 1990).

Because students report high levels of self-efficacy while also reporting high levels of anxiety and chronic sadness, this demonstrates a dangerous combination of students willing to persist with their academics, who have high stress and low familiarity with effective coping mechanisms; thus, students do not successfully know how to cope with their stressors, resorting to using emotion and avoidance coping mechanisms, dwelling on their negative emotions instead of addressing the stressor.

Based on these findings, we recommend that Douglas Valley develop and support the Wellness Center with a full-time Social Worker/Counselor to explicitly teach students healthy coping strategies for life's stressors. We also recommend that Douglas Valley create student groups that engage both student and parent groups to learn more about their needs, as well as specifically engage and educate the parent community about students' mental health and stress.

Key Chapter Learning

Data analysis is a fundamental step in our knowledge production process. We have argued that at the same time we collect we also must organize the data. But we also recognized that when organizing the data, we start analyzing inevitably. Our brain does not compartmentalize this complex process. Here we divided this section, for clarity purposes, into two moments. Data reduction: We first need to reduce data in order for the analysis to be both feasible and rigorous. Chunking up large amounts of data into significant parts is the first step; data then are sliced into meaningful slices; third, cut these into thinner slices down to a granular level, at a point we know these pieces make sense for analysis.

Second, we went over the second moment. Data display: When we have reached this point, we have made important discoveries by way of answering our research question. After we have completed the data analysis and determined the core findings, we need to report the results. We propose two possible ways to organize the findings section of the report. We may want to organize findings by following the research question and its operational questions as the layout for the entire section. Or, we may want to organize findings by following the major emerging themes. At the end of the day, one selects the best outline according to the makeup of our study's end user. What follows is then the issue of how best to present the evidence. For that, we offered a set of different ways to do so: from inspiring quotations to word frequency analysis.

Essential Question

On the basis of what criteria would you present your findings and the related evidence?

Activity

Displaying data:
   We present here an interview from a case involving a group of teachers from Egyptian Middle School. We have entirely analyzed it. As part of a larger effort, you are responsible for writing a short report on this piece of evidence only.
   The research question the team seeks to answer is this: How does social integration work for dual language learners?
Here is your job:

1. Determine how to write the claim involving the two themes.
2. Explain how the two themes (see below) support the claim.
3. Identify the actual text from the interview you may use as evidence.

192 | Community-Owned Knowledge

4. Integrate this evidence to your narrative as necessary.

Analysis map:

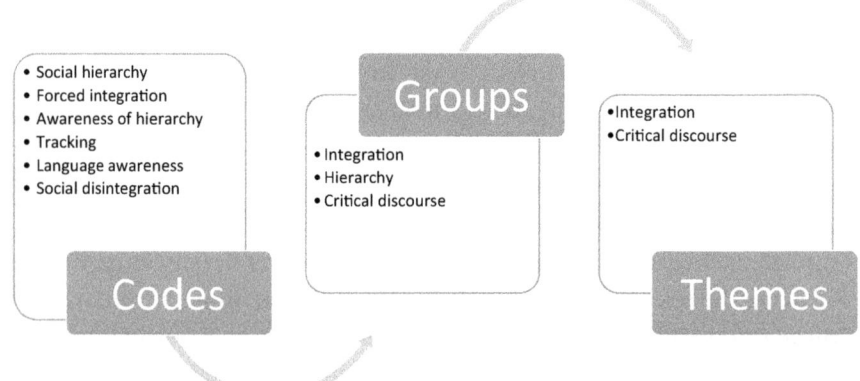

Interviewee: LV (Female, 6th grade English, senior teacher). Egyptian Middle Interviewer: GA. May 14, 2020	Codes	Groups	Themes
GA: Thanks for accepting to participate in this project. LV: Sure			
GA: How's your work with the Latino children in your English 6th grade class? LV: It's OK. But, as you well know, there's a moment when you need to remind yourself that you cannot make a silk purse out of a sow's ear,	Soc. Hierarchy	Integration	Integration
GA: What do you mean? LV: It's an old saying. It is something I heard a few times at my previous middle school in the 80s and 90s when schools were forced to desag [sic] [desegregation] as a result of a consent decree. Kids were bused from downtown.	Forced integ. Awareness of hierarchy	Hierarchy	
GA: And how is it used here at your new site. LV: I've heard the same expression here, at Egyptian, although less so lately. You know, it's about some kids how some have what it takes and some who don't. While I believe it, I'm committed to work hard with the latter.	Tracking		
GA: How? LV: At the macro level, we need to rethink desag [sic]. For instance, some schools became arts magnate as a way to attract students (my comment: from the middle classes). Castle Middle, where I taught for 7 years goes to its feeder elementary schools to recruit the best students. They get kids from downtown and bring them to the south end of the city. The downtown kids would be shocked because competing with the local kids made them losers, since the local kids had been in arts programs for years, and so at the auditions the downtown kids always would lose. They rarely would get into the arts classes they wanted. Yet, Castle school is in "compliance" with desag [sic].	Awareness of hierarchy Tracking Tracking		
GA: And, how does your new school do it? LV: Egyptian, takes anyone with no distinctions. We get kids from 3 elementary: Garner and Lowell where most Latino lower class kids go, and Trace elementary a more middle class population. It is an arts school. While we take anybody, not anybody gets into the arts program. Our graduates go on to Lincoln High, which is an arts magnet school. This school also gets kids from Castle. In short, let's stop these practices and enforce a better distribution of children throughout schools.	Lang awareness	Critical discourse	Critical discourse

Interviewee: LV (Female, 6th grade English, senior teacher). Egyptian Middle Interviewer: GA. May 14, 2020	Codes	Groups	Themes
GA: How are English Lang. learners scheduled? LV: ELDs, are offered only one elective per semester (six weeks each) in sixth grade, and then from there they select a field course to focus on 7th and 8th.	Soc. disintegration		
GA: What's your opinion about that? LV: In my opinion this is tracking. I am teaching literacy at the 2nd level to kids in sixth grade. So, I teach phonics, vocab and basic grammar.	Soc. disintegration		
GA: How do you talk to your students about issues of demeaning language like the expression you used earlier? LV: I talk to them straight up. One day I brought the word "scrap" which, of course, I know how kids use it against each other. It is applied to Sureños as derogatory.	Awareness of hierarchy		
GA: How did they react? LV: The class went wild about the word, but I explained to them the insidiousness of it. Siblings would be split at home between who is Norteño and who is Sureño, you know. Kids embrace these identities depending how they feel in relation to their residency in the US. Things are so bad that some schools are typical Norteño, like Egyptian. Pioneer High a Sureño, Madrone is a Sureño, Lincoln and Sycamore High are Norteño.			
GA: How does the school talk about this issue? LV: We bring organizations, community activist. Conflict mediation folks. We do a lot, but kids still separate.			

Resources

The Agile Research Platform (data analysis platform)
https://alphahq.com/research/
Auto Translate (audio transcription)
https://trint.com/
Tableau (comprehensive data analysis platform)
https://www.tableau.com/
Dedoose (data analysis platform)
https://www.dedoose.com/
Hyper Research (data analysis platform)

http://www.researchware.com/products/hyperresearch.html

Matthew B. Milles, & A. Michael Huberman (1994). *Qualitative data analysis* (2nd ed.). Thousand Oaks, CA: Sage.

Margaret D. LeCompte, & Jean J. Schensul (1999). *Designing and conducting ethnographic research*. Walnut Creek, CA: Altamira Press.

Index

A

Abstracts 100, 113–115, 118, 186
APA style 115, 116, 122, 123, 125–127
Analysis
   integrated disciplines 20
   one-dimensional layer 19, 20, 35, 42
   unit of 40, 138, 188
Argyris, Chris 7, 41, 42
Arguments, convincing 38
Attribution, intrinsic and
     extrinsic 62–64
Attribution fallacies 65–68
   Post hoc 65
   Ad populum 65
   Hasty generalization 65, 66
   Ad hominem 66
   Argument from authority 66
   Red herring 67

B

Bias 12, 23, 31, 38, 39, 61, 97, 101, 102, 132, 142, 143, 155
   control 31, 132, 143
Bourdieu, Pierre 28

C

Capital
   convert 27
   accumulate 27
   exchange 27
   generate 27
   transport 27
Cause and effect 43, 47, 62
Challenge 38, 68, 98

identification 9, 41, 42, 136
manifestation of 41, 49, 136, 186
overt 41–42
Chunking 168, 169, 191
Citations 115, 116, 122, 123
Coaching 32, 154
Codes
   family 172–174
   identical 172
Commitment to move forward 46, 75, 96, 124
Components, input and output 76, 78–81, 87, 90
Consensus
   building 32, 74, 75, 90
   shared concern 15, 39, 75
   mechanism 64
   meaning and definition for team 83
   social 59–61, 96
Consistency across comparable situations 83, 91, 149
Counter-narrative 176, 180
Climate 37
Cultural capital 5, 8, 24, 27, 31, 136
   generating social and cultural capital via CAR 24, 29
   institutional protective agents xix, 29
   static and relational 28, 29, 47
Cycle of inquiry 25, 35, 67

D

Data as a learning catalytic 135
   baseline 55, 57, 70
   reduction 5, 167, 172–175, 191
   using multiple points 85
Databases
   searches 111
   specialized online academic 98, 110, 111
Deductive and inductive arguments 121, 159
Delpit, Lisa 28, 29

Democratization of knowledge 36, 67
Demographics 69, 100, 106, 138, 156, 180, 182
Descriptors 113, 114, 124, 125

E

Endnotes 115
Ethics 140
Evidence
   expertise 4, 60, 61, 66, 67
   social consensus 59–61, 96
Evidentiary material 36, 37, 46, 55, 60, 102, 177

F

Factors 64, 78, 80, 81, 86, 90, 91
   embedded 80, 106
Field notes 117, 130, 139, 141–145
Frequency analysis 60, 183, 184, 191
Functional organizational practice 37, 102

G

Gap analysis 43, 44
Goals and objectives for action research 25, 31, 45, 55, 57, 70, 140
Ground-level questions
   meaning of concepts 83
   operational 86, 88, 91, 97, 140, 185
   precautions with formulating 88
Granular-level items 51–81, 138, 155, 191

H

Habermas, Jürgen 37
Habitus 28, 31

Human resources for action research 54, 56, 58, 96, 124

I

Iceberg model 41
Inside vs. outside 63, 132, 155
Internet search engine 95, 111
Interpret research 113
Interviews, feasibility 97
Itemization 80, 90, 139

J

Journaling 144, 152, 155

L

Language, habituated behaviors and rites 31, 50
Layers, above/below/deeper 42
Leadership capacity 36, 37, 102
Life world 12, 37
Local production 36

M

Multiple disciplines 19, 20
Multiple sources 96, 100, 110, 124
Multiple voices 19, 35, 36, 99, 102, 103, 121

N

Narratives 59, 60, 99, 130, 131, 143, 155, 180, 176, 177

O

Organization Culture 23, 37, 42, 46, 67
Outlier 172, 173, 175
Ownership of knowledge 5, 11, 35, 36, 140

Q

Question Design 82, 83, 85, 86, 90, 91, 103
Questionnaire 100, 103, 105, 106, 117, 139, 149, 151, 152
Questions
  alignment 55, 84
  closed and open-ended 86, 87, 89, 91, 106, 151, 152
  objective and subjective 83, 84, 86, 91
  measurable data points 55, 84
  operationalize a systematic way to answer step-by-step 83, 90, 91
  quantifying characteristics 91, 183
  what-How to uncover new information 76, 169
Quick notes 142, 143, 155

R

References, how to write 115, 118
Reliability 61, 82, 86, 91, 103, 132, 133, 149, 155
Relationships xix, 4, 15, 24, 27, 32, 33, 35, 36, 50, 149, 152, 189
Research questions
  formulating 74, 77, 82, 86–88, 90
  synthesizing the challenge 96
  guiding the research project 99
Researcher practitioner 36, 103
Revising
  editing 119–123
  e-reading themes 123

S

Salient features 116, 121, 138, 183, 186
Sampling approaches
  convenience (random) 57, 137
  quota (non-random) 138
Scope boundaries 39, 44, 64
Selection criteria 112, 133, 136, 137
Seminal publications 104, 111, 115, 121
Shadowing 134, 139, 153–155
Social capital 27, 28, 31
Social connectivity 21
Social networks 1, 4, 5, 27, 28, 31, 50, 66, 137
Sources
  credibility level 100
  credentials' legitimacy 61, 100–102
  factual accuracy 101, 125
Sources of information
  primary 5, 103–105, 107–109, 124, 132
  secondary 103, 104, 108, 132
Structures xvii 5, 37, 50, 67, 79–81, 102, 186
Studies
  empirical 61, 107, 125
  qualitative 117, 132
  quantitative 117
  theoretical 61, 107, 126, 186
Substantiating claims 38, 52, 59, 102, 121, 122, 175, 185
System world 37

T

Target audience 38, 40, 175, 186
Testimonios/Testimonies 58, 98–100, 107, 132
Theory of action 24, 54, 56, 58, 70
Timeline 43, 48, 54, 70

Tracking authors' definitions 109, 172, 174, 175
Triangulation 66, 83, 85, 86, 122, 133, 134, 152, 153

U

Unexpected discovery 166, 172, 173, 175
Unit of analysis. *See* Analysis, unit of
University librarians' role 110–113

V

Validity 61, 82, 85, 86, 91, 103, 132, 133, 135, 149, 155
Variables
  governing 9, 26, 41, 42, 49
  independent and dependent 78–80, 85, 87, 90, 117, 121
Vignette, definition 179

W

Writing the Literature Review 62, 96, 98, 103–105, 107, 109, 124
  drafting 119–123
  duplicative information 97
  mechanics 84, 119, 123
  planning and organizing 119, 134, 166
  re-reading themes 123
  topic sentences 121, 122

Z

Zero point 36

www.ingramcontent.com/pod-product-compliance
Ingram Content Group UK Ltd.
Pitfield, Milton Keynes, MK11 3LW, UK
UKHW021835210426
5322IPUK00018B/271